True Crime

Storytime

12 Disturbing True Crime Stories to Keep You Up All Night

True Crime Storytime Volume 5

M. Moore, True Crime Seven

TRUE CRIME Z

ISBN: 9798842668991

Table of Contents

Explore the Stories of

The Murderous Minds

A Note

From True Crime Seven

Hi there!

Thank you so much for picking up our book! Before you continue your exploration into the dark world of killers, we wanted to take a quick moment to explain the purpose of our books.

Our goal is to simply explore and tell the stories of various killers in the world: from unknown murderers to infamous serial killers. Our books are designed to be short and inclusive; we want to tell a good scary true story that anyone can enjoy regardless of their reading level.

That is why you won't see too many fancy words or complicated sentence structures in our books. Also, to prevent typical cut and dry style of true crime books, we try to keep the narrative easy to follow while incorporating fiction style storytelling. As to information, we often find ourselves with too little or too much. So, in terms of research material and content, we always try to include what further helps the story of the killer.

Lastly, we want to acknowledge that, much like history, true crime is a subject that can often be interpreted differently. Depending on the topic and your upbringing, you might agree or disagree with how we present a story. We understand disagreements are inevitable. That is why we added this note so hopefully it can help you better understand our position and goal.

Now without further ado, let the exploration to the dark begin!

Introduction

WHAT COMES TO MIND WHEN YOU THINK OF the 1960s? Probably iconic bands like The Beatles, popular trends such as lava lamps and miniskirts, and more likely than not, all things Bohemian. However, this is the preferred happy, peaceful, and pleasant view of the decade. If you are willing to take off the rose-colored-glasses for a moment, I would like to introduce you to the more sinister side of the sixties.

Crime rose exponentially during this period. Though it is hard for historians to pinpoint why, whether it be a change in cultural norms or blatant stratifications of society, one thing is for sure – every crime, from robbery to rape, skyrocketed, including murder.

The 1960s saw a wave of mass murders in the United States. In other countries, like Australia, they were facing novel crimes as well, such as the first child kidnapping for ransom. It seemed no corner of the globe was immune to the darkest desires of some of humanity's most foul. People like:

Richard Speck: A bloodthirsty killer who, when he was down and out on his luck, thought killing a dormitory of young nurses might be the answer to his problem.

Sharon Elizabeth Kinne: A clever and conniving housewife who would do whatever it took to achieve her dreams, even if it meant ruthlessly killing anyone who stood in her way and framing those who dared to go against her.

John Norman Collins: A college student who couldn't help but murder his co-ed classmates, usually in the most brutal ways, before dumping their bodies to be discovered by unsuspecting citizens.

The Robinson Family: A family vacation gone very wrong, where they returned not sunburnt and satisfied but in body bags.

Mysterious and hair-raising, these true stories of murder and mayhem will keep you guessing. We worked hard to put together the facts precisely as they have been recorded, allowing you to come to your own conclusions about these chilling crimes. To do so, you will need to dive deep into the bloodcurdling details and woeful witness statements.

Are you ready to ponder the psyche of a killer?

I

The Ypsilanti Ripper

THE MOTTO "TUNE IN, DROP OUT" MAY HAVE
been popular in the sixties, but college campuses were
booming. However, the student body was still predominantly
male, white, and affluent. Many campuses were co-ed, but women
were the minority. It could have been this undercurrent of male
superiority that fueled a campus killer named John Norman
Collins.

Raised with rotating father figures and homes filled with
domestic violence, he developed some sinister traits – particularly
narcissism, chauvinism, and necrophilia. However, John was a
master at concealing these characteristics, allowing him to hide in

plain sight as he preyed on the co-eds of Eastern Michigan University.

A Cold-Blooded Killing of a Co-Ed

Mary Fleszar's roommate was worried. Mary, a fellow nineteen-year-old college student and friend, had not returned home in over twenty-four hours. Eastern Michigan University had its fair share of parties that could stretch from one day into the next. Still, it wasn't like Mary to simply vanish. So, on July 18, 1967, she contacted Mary's parents, who promptly notified the police. After a quick review of the apartment, the police noted that all of Mary's possessions were left behind, making it unlikely that she had planned to leave for any length of time.

A neighbor recalled a blue-gray Chevrolet approaching Mary not long before her disappearance. Mary had been out for a walk in an unmistakable bright orange tent dress covered with bold white polka dots. As she was nearing her apartment, the male driver stopped alongside her and seemed to ask her a question. The small, five-foot-two girl shook her head, pushed her glasses up her slender nose, and continued walking. Not even two minutes later, the same scene played over again, except this time, when Mary shook her head, the driver drove off angrily, screeching his tires as he backed out. The neighbor had found the exchange mildly concerning but lost sight of Mary as she continued around the corner.

Russell Crisovan Jr. and Mark Lucas, both fifteen, had heard the reports of the missing girl. Russell's father owned a farm not far from campus. A month after Mary's disappearance, they were getting ready to plow a field when they heard a car door slam, then another. Making their way toward the sound, believing they were about to catch a pair of secretive lovers in the act, the boys were startled to find nothing but fresh tire tracks and a stomach-turning smell. A leathery mass with blackened skin appeared to be the source of the odor. Creeping closer to the decomposing carcass, Russell and Mark noticed the maggots and flies burrowing into it, the stench suspended in the hot summer air. One of them leaned in for a closer inspection. His eyes grew wide when he made out a familiar shape on the lumpy, unrecognizable head – a human ear.

State Police immediately identified the corpse as human, though it was missing quite a few parts and was in a severe state of decomposition. The body lay on its side, stripped of clothing, missing one forearm and hand, the fingers of the opposite hand, and both feet. A later autopsy would reveal that this body was that of a female who had been dead around one month. Her remains appeared to have significant bruising, blunt force trauma, and various animal bites and claw marks. Thirty stab wounds, twenty of them from a knife or sharp object, covered her chest. Her lower leg bones, where both feet had been severed, were shattered just above the ankles.

The crime scene, which was the site of an old farmhouse at the end of the road, held more clues. The body had been moved three times, either by the killer or by scavenging animals. First, it lay on top of a heap of bottles and cans before moving five feet south, then three more feet. The tire tracks of the car the boys heard had pulled up right alongside where the body lay, indicating that whoever it was had only one objective that day – to see her.

A discarded leather sandal, a vibrant orange and polka dot dress under some trash, and dental records were all identified as belonging to Mary Fleszar. A man arrived at the parlor just before her funeral, parking his bluish-gray Chevy right out front. He told the director that he was a family friend and had come to view Mary one last time. However, he wanted to take a picture of the corpse as a keepsake for her parents.

The director steadfastly refused, to which the man replied, "You mean you can't fix her up enough so I can at least get one picture of her?" Again, the director told him this was impossible. The man stormed off, leaving the director to recall only later that he didn't even have a camera with him. When he brought it up to the Fleszars later, they said they had never met such a person. He never returned to the burial or the funeral, leaving police to believe that the mysterious photographer was probably their murderer.

The Michigan Murders

Mary would be the first in a series of at least seven murders. The second victim didn't appear until a year after Mary's burial.

On July 2, 1968, the roommate of twenty-year-old Eastern student Joan Schell was experiencing a similar situation as Mary's roommate. Joan had gone out for a walk and had not returned. Joan's parents and the police were alerted, but they wouldn't have to wait long to discover what happened to the young woman. Five days later, a construction crew in Ann Arbor discovered Joan's body at their worksite. She had been raped, beaten, and was left decomposing in the summer sun. Like Mary, Joan had been stabbed at least forty-seven times by a sharp object. Her time of death was close to her disappearance, but the killer had dumped her body at the worksite less than twenty-four hours before its discovery.

However, this time, police had more to go on than just a vehicle description. Two friends of Joan's reported that they saw her walking with another Eastern Michigan University student by the name of John Norman Collins. Collins lived right across the street from Joan at 619 Emmett in Ypsilanti. Police were quick to question him. The personable and clean-cut John told officers that he was at his mother's house in Center Line, Michigan, the night of the disappearance. Satisfied with this alibi, investigators took his word and left.

Nine months later, yet another co-ed was found. Jane Mixer lay in Denton Cemetery, a few miles outside Ypsilanti. She hadn't attended Eastern but the nearby University of Michigan in Ann Arbor. Her body wasn't riddled with stab wounds but possessed a single bullet hole. In addition, she had been strangled, and the killer had positioned the novel Catch-22 along with her shoes at her side. The police were confounded; in some ways, this case matched the details of the recent slayings, but there were marked differences.

That same month a younger girl would meet a similar fate. Beaten to death, sixteen-year-old Maralynn Skelton was discovered soon after. Friends told police that she frequented an apartment that happened to be next door to an apartment owned by a male Eastern Michigan University student. That student was good friends with none other than John Collins, who had been seen spending time there. The ferocity with which Maralynn was attacked appalled the police. Not only had her skull been crushed, but she had been sexually assaulted with a stick, and her body appeared to show signs of flogging.

A few weeks later, the body count increased while the victim's age decreased; thirteen-year-old Dawn Basom was found half-naked, strangled, with an electric cord still wrapped around her throat, her body discarded in a field. Dawn had last been seen walking alone down a dirt road. John Collins was spotted riding his motorcycle up and down the same dirt road.

A nearby abandoned farmhouse turned up the girl's sweater. When police returned to search the house again a few weeks later, they would find more women's clothing not belonging to Dawn.

A little less than a month later, the house was mysteriously set ablaze.

As if the public wasn't incensed enough, not long after the teen's murder, yet another body of a young girl was stumbled upon by a pair of teenage boys roaming through an empty field. University of Michigan graduate student Alice Kalom had been stabbed, shot, and had her throat violently cut.

As spring turned to summer, tensions were rising. Investigators had no killer, much less any leads, and the body count continued to climb. July 23, 1969 – a situation all too familiar to police played out once again. Student Karen Sue Beineman had gone missing. She had been seen leaving her dorm and heading to a wig shop.

Inside the shop, she told the store owner, "I've just done the most foolish thing of my life, accepted a ride from a total stranger." Outside, a handsome man sat astride a Triumph motorcycle waiting for Karen.

A witness told police that the same man on the motorcycle had offered her a ride, but she had refused. It was a shame Karen hadn't done the same. In a wooded gully, her body was found – strangled and beaten. Her chest and stomach were scalded by a caustic liquid. Her underwear had been crumpled and shoved inside her; they were covered with short hairs not belonging to the victim.

A Break in the Brutal Case

State Police Corporal David Leik and his family returned home to Ypsilanti three days later. His wife's nephew, John Collins, had agreed to house-sit for him, and Leik was not impressed. Black paint splashes dotted his basement floor. Checking back into work the following day, his wife's nephew came up again, this time as a questioned suspect in the co-ed killing spree.

Leik painstakingly scraped up the black paint in his basement, uncovering brown spots beneath. Lab analysis proved the stains were simply varnish, but it turned out investigators didn't need them as incriminating evidence. When Leik moved the washing machine to clear the final paint stains, he found hair clippings, mistakenly swept under the machine from the family's haircuts before vacation. Forensics found that these clippings were identical to those on Karen's underwear. The slain college student had been in Leik's basement.

Chillingly Charming

John was born in Ontario, Canada, to Richard and Loretta Chapman. However, Richard wouldn't stick around for long. Within John's first nine years of life, he would be introduced to three father figures, almost all of them fond of domestic violence. Despite a tumultuous upbringing, John did well in school. He was a good-looking kid with quite a few friends, often described as an "All American Boy." His teachers praised him for his hard work and academic skills, referring to him as bright and gifted. All his efforts paid off when he was accepted to Eastern Michigan University in the fall of 1966.

Eastern was nestled in the small town of Ypsilanti, Michigan. Just outside of Ann Arbor, it boasted a beautiful landscape and a hometown feel. After arriving at the University, John quickly joined the Theta Chi fraternity house. But his "All American" facade rapidly cracked. His grades slipped, he hung around the wrong crowds, and became involved in petty theft. After more than one incident, Theta Chi kicked him out. John then rented an apartment in a house one block south of the campus. Aside from his minor crimes, he was well-liked around campus. The personable, clean-cut, and charming young man told his professors that he was studying to become a teacher.

But it was his extracurriculars that concerned the police. With the damning evidence of the hair clippings, they quickly arrested John Collins for the murders of the slain girls. Though he denied all involvement, authorities uncovered suspicious events from his past. Not only was he a chronic thief, but he had a penchant for violence against women.

Once, as a teen, he found his pregnant and married sister with another man. He beat her so severely that she had to be hospitalized. Others who knew him said he had been long obsessed with gore and mutilation and was known to harass women sexually. Witnesses were effortlessly able to positively identify John. From the girl he had offered a ride to before picking up Karen to the wig store owner, they instantly recognized him. Leik's neighbor reported hearing strange sounds coming from the home prior to Karen's death and seeing John leave with a large laundry detergent box the following day. John's roommate noted to police that he had seen the same box in John's room — containing miscellaneous female belongings.

Conviction of the Co-ed Killer

A jury swiftly moved to find John guilty of Karen's murder – sentencing him to life in prison without the possibility of parole. He was also named in a grand jury indictment in a case in Monterrey, California. Shortly after killing Alice Kalom, he had offered a ride to young Roxie Phillips, who was on her way to mail a letter when he was vacationing there. Her tortured and mutilated body turned up in Monterrey Bay several days later. A scrap of fabric matching the dress she was last seen wearing was found inside John's car.

John is cited with killing at least seven girls, though some believe the count is much higher. Jane Mixer, the victim from the cemetery, is not accredited to John Collins. In 2005, a former nurse by the name of Gary Leiterman was convicted of her murder.

Nevertheless, the Ypsilanti-Ripper, now known as John Norman Chapman after a name change, terrified the university town in the 1960s. Preying on young female students while hiding in plain sight as a charming and clean-cut college student.

II

The Murders at Starved Rock

THREE WOMEN SET OFF FOR STARVED ROCK State Park. The middle-aged socialites sought a break from their families and mundane housewifely duties, deciding to escape to the rugged and rural Starved Rock State Park. Unfortunately, their idyllic vacation would quickly descend into a vicious nightmare. This story hasn't gotten any clearer with age, and if anything, it has become more convoluted. Causing all involved to wonder – was the Starved Rock Slayer ever really caught?

A Gruesome Girls Getaway

Three Chicago women were headed out for a relaxing girl's trip in March 1960 in Utica, Illinois. The first member of the trio was Lillian Oding, an immigrant from Ireland who had come over to Illinois as a child and was now forty-nine. Unlike Lillian, Frankie, or Francis, Murphy had lived in Illinois all her life. The forty-seven-year-old was a local to Farmington, Illinois, and very familiar with the area. Mildred Lindquist was the final member; at fifty-three, she was the oldest and had spent all her years in nearby Chicago. The suburban women lived near the city and were all well-known and respected in their communities, having been married to elite Chicago business executives.

All three had children and homes to take care of, but on Sunday, March 13th, they decided to break free from their dull routine. Meeting at their church, Riverside Presbyterian, Lillian, Frankie, and Mildred agreed there was no better time than the present. On the following day, they would pack up and leave. The destination was somewhere physically close but far removed from their daily experiences – Starved Rock State Park. It was just under two hours away but boasted raw nature and gorgeous accommodations. Not wanting to abandon their families, the women went grocery shopping that afternoon, purchasing enough necessities to fill the fridges for the coming week.

It had been a particularly rough winter for Lillian's husband, George. He battled poor health as a result of a heart condition. Lillian needed a break, but she worried about her spouse. On Monday morning, March 14th, Lillian promised her husband she would call to check in on him every evening she was away. With a quick kiss on the cheek, the beautiful middle-aged socialite departed in Frankie's gray station wagon. As their car rumbled up the rural road in Utica, the women were awestruck.

In front of them stood the rustic lodge in all its splendor, surrounded by a forest blanketed in early spring snow. Lillian, Frankie, and Mildred were given two rooms in which to stay. Lillian would remain alone in room 109, and the other two agreed to bunk in adjoining room 110. After grabbing the keys from Esther, the front desk clerk, the three rushed to their accommodations, doing nothing more than discarding their bags just inside the door before heading to the dining room. Over lunch, they decided that there was still enough light in the day for a short hike. Near the lodge was an easy, one-mile trail, the perfect length for an afternoon excursion. The ladies put on coats, boots, and long woolen skirts. Frankie grabbed her camera, and another woman stuck a pair of binoculars in her pocket; then, they headed out to the trail.

When late Monday evening rolled around, George was surprised to have not heard from Lillian. He decided to give her a call before he turned in for bed. Calling the front desk of the Starved Rock Lodge, he was quickly put through to room 109. The phone rang repeatedly before the operator routed his call back to the front desk. The attendant reassured George that the women were likely enjoying a late dinner, mentioning that they had checked in earlier, ate a light lunch, and said they were heading out for a brisk hike. Satisfied, George signed off and expected his wife would call tomorrow.

The following day, on March 15th, a postcard arrived for Lillian, Frankie, and Mildred. Esther slipped the message from the ladies' dear friend, wishing them well on their trip, into box 109. Not long after, the phone rang. It was George, again asking for Lillian; he was now a bit perturbed that he had not heard from his wife. Another employee again placated the worried husband, telling him that the three women were spotted at breakfast not an hour ago and had been seen leaving the lodge shortly after.

Only that wasn't the truth – no one had seen the women. Confident in his wife's whereabouts, George should have been anything but calm. He should have been very, very concerned.

The Snow was Stained red

That evening, a blizzard rolled in. While the guests hunkered down inside the lodge, a blanket of frozen white built up; in the end, the storm would deposit a few inches on the Starved Rock State Park. On Wednesday, when George called, he demanded to talk to Lillian. Not hearing from her on Monday was understandable; it was a little concerning but irritating on Tuesday; now, it was worrisome.

The front desk clerk hustled off to rooms 109 and 110. As the door was pushed open, it came into contact with the women's suitcases, unopened and haphazardly discarded as if they had just dropped them off. The beds were unslept in, the dressers untouched, and the bathroom spotless – Lillian, Frankie, and Mildred were nowhere in sight.

A manager snapped at the clerk to check the parking lot, where Frankie's car sat just as it had when it arrived, covered in snow from the earlier storm. George was frantic. It would appear that his wife and her friends had been missing almost two days, caught out on the trails during a frigid late-season snow.

Esther, arriving for her shift, told the manager that she, too, thought the women had just been in the dining room or out enjoying nature. After all, the postcard she left in their box on Tuesday morning was gone, and she assumed they had picked it up. A maid testified to finding two wet towels, a wet soap bar, and a fresh dirt ring in the tub in room 109 that morning.

George had a horrible gut feeling. He rang his good friend, Virgil, director of the Chicago Crime Commission, an organization that assisted authorities in Chicago. Within the hour, the LaSalle County Sheriff's office was alerted to the disappearances at Starved Rock State Park. Not long after George arrived at the outpost, search parties were organized to find the missing women. Men grouped around, listening for instruction when suddenly, the phone rang.

Up at Starved Rock State Park, a reporter named Bill Danley had gotten word of the case and decided to make a trip up, hoping to be the first on the scene. He got more than he bargained for when a group of boys burst forth from the trailhead. Breathlessly, they told the shocked journalist that there were dead bodies in a

35

cave just up the trail. When Bill phoned it into the lodge, both media and law enforcement officers rapidly descended on the scene.

Near the end of the mile-long trail, a ledge sat only a fifteen-minute jaunt from the start. It barely protruded from the rock face and was more of a shallow cavern than a cave. Police cautiously made their way up the trail. Six inches of snow now covered the ground, and if they hoped to find any shred of evidence, they needed to be careful where they stepped. However, police needn't have worried about mistakenly covering clues – up near the cavern, the once pure, white snow was now blood red.

The bodies of Lillian, Frankie, and Mildred lay side by side on their backs on the cold, hard rock. They were partially nude, their legs askew, and their thighs covered in deep purple bruises. Nearby, a heavy tree branch was so thoroughly coated in blood that it could only be the murder weapon. Twine was wrapped around two of the women's wrists; their bloody and discarded camera and binoculars were found a few feet away. The autopsy revealed that each woman had suffered at least one-hundred blows to their head and chest. This horrific event befell them almost immediately after lunch when they had been on the trail for only fifteen to twenty minutes.

Hunt for the Starved Rock Slayer

Police immediately set their sights on the lodge and its employees and guests. More than five hundred individuals were fingerprinted, and dozens sat for a polygraph test, with no conclusive outcome. Snow had covered any footprints and likely obscured all other pieces of vital evidence. To make matters worse, the local sheriff's office was underfunded and had little resources and finances to devote to the case. Guests checked out with haste, reservations were canceled, and the area was on high alert for a violent, sexually-deviant maniac. Yet only Harold Warren, the LaSalle County State Attorney, was left piecing together the clues.

He purchased a microscope with his own money and spent hours poring over the twine used to bind the women. He found that the two cords were different; one was a twelve ply and the other twenty. Armed with this information, he tracked down identical twine at the lodge, used in their kitchen, going so far as to verify the match with the cord manufacturer. Eventually, the trail of breadcrumbs led him to a kitchen dishwasher.

A polygraph specialist had tested all employees who worked the week of the murder. One man's testimony, in particular, had drained all color from his face. He told Harold; Chester Weger is definitely your man. The former Marine, a young husband and father, had arrived to work the day following the murder bearing deep scratches on his face. More incriminating evidence was uncovered, like the human blood stains on his buckskin jacket.

It wasn't Chester's first time dealing with the authorities. Police had been digging around the year before when a girl was raped and robbed a mile from the lodge. She and her boyfriend had both been tied up with twine. Harold, ever the enterprising detective, found the victim and had her sift through photographs. When she came upon Chester's, her response mirrored the polygraph specialist's – that's your man.

An odd series of factors prohibited authorities from arresting Chester on the spot. Harold was up for re-election and worried that a quick arrest would be fodder for his opponent, who might tell the public that Harold only made the arrest to boost his votes. Furthermore, Harold didn't want Chester to stand for rape and robbery – he was after murder charges. Harold lost the re-election anyway and, with the little time he had left, was spurred into action. Arresting Chester for rape and robbery, under the guise of luring him to the police station with the excuse of further questioning, police probed him about the murders.

Chester blurted, "All right, I got scared. I tried to grab their pocketbook, they fought back, and then I hit them." No purses, pocketbooks, money, or jewelry were carried with the women on their hike; they were all found in the trio's rooms. The brutality of the murder, bludgeoned over one hundred times each, didn't point toward a simple robbery gone wrong. Chester went on to confess that he had tried to run away, but one of the women chased him and hit him with her binoculars; at that point, he picked up the heavy branch. After his rage-fueled attack, an airplane passing overhead prompted him to move the bodies under the ledge. Twice he confessed and even signed a written statement – until he was paired with an attorney. Then, he vehemently denied the murders.

On January 20, 1961, almost one year after Lillian, Frankie, and Mildred were viciously killed on their holiday, Chester was slated to stand trial. On March 4, 1961, Chester Weger was found guilty of both rape and murder. Unfortunately, the jurors, unaware that life in prison meant a chance for parole, spared him the death penalty.

Locked up at twenty-two, Chester would apply for parole more than twenty-four times while in the Stateville Penitentiary.

Two decades later, a woman on her deathbed requested the presence of a police sergeant. When he arrived, she said she wanted to clear her conscience, retelling an incident at a "State Park" when she was younger in which a situation concerning her and her friends got out of control, leading to multiple victims whose bodies had to be dragged. Her daughter prohibited her from saying any more, citing her mother's "insanity." Nothing ever came from the deathbed confession, but Chester maintained his innocence.

As the years went on, the inaccuracy of polygraphs has come to light, as have the less-than-legal interrogation techniques of police officers in the 1960s. With these pieces of evidence on their side, Chester's lawyers succeeded in getting him paroled on February 21, 2020.

Eighty-four-year-old Chester gave an interview denouncing his involvement in the murders and his hopes to move to the suburbs and meet his almost sixty-year-old daughter. She was only one at the time of his incarceration.

Did Chester serve his time, or was it never his to serve? The missing postcard and the wet towels were left unexplained. Solid evidence against Chester was never found, though conclusions were made. Unfortunately, assumptions often don't provide closure.

III

Richard Speck

THE 1960S WERE LARGELY STILL AN AGE OF innocence, in that mass murders hadn't really occurred in previous decades. Society wasn't regularly gripped with fear after hearing of senseless mass killings. There had been infrequent shootings with victims approaching the double digits since before the twentieth century. Still, the 1960s would bring about something different. A more disturbing, insensible type of killing with increasingly more significant body counts. Cases such as the horrible crimes of the Texas Tower Shooting, the Zodiac killer, Ted Bundy, and the infamous Richard Speck as examples.

A Tumultuous Upbringing

In 1941, the village of Kirkwood, Illinois, welcomed a new resident – Richard Speck. Young Richard didn't really stand out, being the seventh child in a family of eight. However, he and his six older siblings had a ten-plus-year age gap. His parents were deeply religious, hardworking, and had strict moral values. Most notably, no drinking of any kind. For a while, the family lived an uneventful life; but a move to Monmouth, Illinois, would be the first of many changes for Richard. Shortly after the move, his father passed away at fifty-three, when Richard was only six. Then, not long after, his older brother passed away at twenty-five. Losing a father and a father figure was hard on Richard, but things were only about to worsen.

Richard's mother met a man by the name of Carl Lindbergh. Carl had a penchant for drinking that would have likely explained his criminal record that spanned twenty-five years. His long list of charges included fraud, drunk driving, and abuse. He was nothing like Richard's father, who was loving, hardworking, and morally upright in every sense of the word. That didn't stop Richard's mother from marrying Carl, however, and the family of four moved to Texas to be with their new stepfather, leaving the older, now settled siblings back in Illinois.

Carl didn't provide for Richard's mother or her two youngest children. Many of the homes they moved to were rundown and located in poor areas. Richard's new stepfather wasn't emotionally supportive either, often verbally and physically abusing Richard and his sister during his drunken binges. Life outside the Speck home wasn't much better. Richard was a relatively poor student and mostly kept to himself. By twelve, Richard had taken up drinking like his dear old stepfather. Richard's peers believed that he was drunk nearly every day in high school. He eventually dropped out at sixteen.

Another trait of Carl's that Richard seemed to inherit was a penchant for crime. At thirteen, young Richard was picked up for trespassing. From there, the misdemeanors continued to pile up, including breaking and entering, drug charges, and disturbing the peace. By the age of twenty-four, Richard was arrested at least forty-one times.

All the while, Richard was working at a local Dallas company. On his trips to and from work, he met fifteen-year-old Shirley Malone. The pair quickly began dating, and Shirley was pregnant in the blink of an eye. In January 1962, the couple was married. They moved in with Richard's mom, his younger sister, Carolyn, and her husband. Thankfully, Carl was no longer in the picture. But he had left a lasting impression on Richard. The teenager was emotionally abusive to his wife, often pulling up to the house with prostitutes and fondling them in Shirley's sight before driving away. During this time, Richard served a sixteen-month prison sentence for aggravated assault and an additional six-month sentence for attacking a woman in a parking lot with a seventeen-inch knife. When the pair eventually separated in 1966, Shirley claimed that Richard had raped her more than once at knifepoint.

Despite this accusation and Richard's numerous charges of aggravated assault, his mother would hire a lawyer to get her son off the hook for every charge.

When Richard wasn't drinking, he was timid, anxious, and refused to speak to anyone due to nerves. But as soon as he had alcohol in his system: "He will fight or threaten anybody as long as he has a knife or a gun," reported his probation officer.

A Liquor-Fueled Lust for Blood

After the divorce from his wife, Richard moved back to Monmouth to live with his sister. It didn't matter the geographic location; if there was alcohol to be had, Richard would use it to fuel his drunken crime sprees. Not long after moving, he stabbed a man, stole a car, robbed a grocery store, and finally tortured and raped a sixty-five-year-old woman before burglarizing her house. Next, he killed a thirty-two-year-old waitress at a bar where he was performing some manual labor. Her name was Mary Kay Pierce. Her corpse was discovered a few days later with a ruptured liver that authorities believed resulted from a massive blow to her stomach. Police questioned Richard, a regular bar patron. Just when his crimes were about to catch up with him, he skipped town to another sister's house.

To say that he outstayed his welcome would be an understatement. After moving in and terrorizing the community, his siblings wanted nothing to do with him. With nowhere left to turn, he enlisted with the National Maritime Union.

On July 12th, Richard was given his first assignment, only to find it passed on to another crew member just moments after arriving at the dock. Now, he was indeed out of time and money –

the walls were closing in. He turned to the only constant in his life, alcohol.

Living up to his probation officer's file notes, Richard was looking for a fight. First, though, he needed a weapon. Ella Mae Hooper was a fifty-three-year-old woman who happened to be drinking in the same Chicago tavern as Richard that day. He had a switchblade on him, so he held her up and forced her into his room. There, he raped her and was delighted to find a .22 caliber Rohm pistol when he searched her purse.

Armed with more than a blade, Richard was ready to embark on his liquor-fueled blood lust spree. Stumbling through the streets of Chicago's south side, he began looking for someone, *anyone*, to take his rage out on.

On the night of July 12, 1966, he set his sights on a well-kept, nicer-looking townhouse at 2319 East 100 Street. It wasn't a family home but the dormitory for nine student nurses attending the South Chicago Community Hospital.

Richard knocked on the door violently. After the fourth knock, Corazon Amurao, who went by Cora, answered. As soon as she set her eyes on gangly, pockmarked, and haggard-looking Richard, she immediately moved to shut the door, but not before

47

glimpsing the gun in his hand. Unfortunately, Cora wasn't fast enough.

Richard pushed his way inside and immediately grabbed Cora, hissing, "Where are your companions?" Merlita Gargullo and Valentina Pasion, fellow exchange students from the Philippines, were woken by the loud banging on the door. As they made their way downstairs, Richard instantly apprehended both women. The three were hauled into a large bedroom at the rear of the house, where Patricia Matusek, Pamela Wilkening, and Nina Jo Schmale were asleep in their beds.

Merlita, Valentina, and Cora saw it as their opportunity to escape, fleeing to a closet and hiding inside. Richard proceeded to wake the women from their beds, threatening them with the gun. One of the women approached the exchange students in the closet and more or less begged the girls to come out, telling them that he only wanted their valuables and wasn't going to harm them. Slowly, they exited their hiding place and joined the other women in the semi-circle they had formed on the floor. Richard sat down in front of the group.

He began talking to them in a calm voice. One by one, the women got up to retrieve their purses and handed over all the cash that they had. Not long after Richard had pocketed the last nurse's dollars, the front door quietly opened and then slipped shut. It was Gloria Jean Davy, who had been out on a date with her boyfriend when Richard arrived. Slightly inebriated, she was confused to find her roommates sitting on their bedroom floor at gunpoint. Cautiously, Gloria joined the circle as Richard stood and moved to one of the beds.

Methodically, he cut strips from the bedsheet, hanging them around his neck as his knife sliced off fabric piece after piece. Next, Richard took the twelve strips and bound all nurses at their wrists and ankles. Mary Ann Jordan and Suzanne Farris were the last to return home that night and walk in on the disturbing scene. When they entered their bedroom, Richard was standing over Pamela, who was bound and gagged, her eyes pleading with Mary Ann and Suzanne's. Terrified, the two newcomers screamed and raced down the hallway, Richard close behind. He captured them as they made their way to the door, hauling them into another bedroom. The women clawed at their attacker, only to be met with Richard's knife. He stabbed and strangled them until their bodies lost all fight. When satisfied, he washed all the blood off in the bathroom before returning to Pamela.

49

Richard stabbed Pamela with one swift blow, plunging the blade directly into her heart. Over the course of hours, he took the women one by one and sexually assaulted or raped them before stabbing and strangling them. As Richard claimed his victims, it became evident to the bound and waiting nurses what was happening to their friends. Some attempted to hide. Cora was one such person, shimmying her way underneath a bunk bed. Nina Schmale was led away next to be stabbed in the neck and suffocated by a pillow. Cora knew that when she heard the bathroom faucet turn on, Richard would soon be coming back.

Valentina was his next victim; she was quickly dispatched, and again Richard went to the bathroom. Over and over, Cora watched and heard her friends being taken away and begging for their life before being murdered. Pat was punched in the stomach, receiving the same ruptured liver as one of Richard's earlier victims. Gloria was one of the final victims, raped in sight of Cora. The latter was hiding beneath the bed before she was assaulted and finally killed downstairs.

Alone upstairs, Cora crawled across the floor to another bed, concealing herself behind a blanket that was draped off the mattress. Silently, she watched as Richard once again entered the room. This time, he dumped out the women's purses on the floor

50

where they had all been seated not too long ago. He pocketed all valuables before hurriedly exiting the room, making his way down the stairs, and leaving the townhouse. Afraid to move, Cora remained under the bed for nearly two more hours until an alarm clock broke the silence that had descended on the mass murder scene. It was five in the morning.

Richard on the run

Cora untied her ankles and wrists, only to have to pass a trail of bodies, the corpses of her friends and classmates, on the way to her bedroom. There, she climbed to her top bunk and began shouting out the window. Eventually, dislodging the screen, stepping out onto the ledge, and desperately screaming at the top of her lungs for help.

A neighbor exited her home to find Cora screaming, "They're all dead!" The neighbor immediately called the police. The authorities discovered fingerprints that were turned over to the FBI. Every person and business in the area was questioned. One of them was the nearby shipyard where Richard had been denied placement earlier that day. From these records and Cora's description, the police quickly matched Richard's fingerprints to those discovered in the nurses' townhouse.

On July 16th, the media shared the investigator's announcement that they were officially looking for a man by the name of Richard Speck in relation to the mass murder of the eight nursing students. Richard was drinking in a nearby bar, accompanied by a group of people and a stack of newspapers detailing the killings that he had picked up earlier in the day. One of those people, Claude Lundsford, recognized Richard and called the police to report the killer's location.

Unfortunately, the police never investigated the report. It wouldn't be until later that night that police would arrive, called into the hospital to check out an attempted suicide patient. The man was none other than Richard himself, who had broken a beer bottle and gouged his wrists and arms. At the hospital, a resident had recognized his "Born to Raise Hell" tattoo described to the police by Cora and called it in. Richard was arrested after a brief, two-day-long manhunt.

A psychiatrist declared him fit for trial, and his case went in front of a judge on April 3, 1967. He told the jury that he had no recollection of the murders. The prosecution presented a positive witness identification, the knife with his fingerprints collected from the crime scene, t-shirts of his covered in the victim's blood, and sperm from the victims that matched Richard's DNA. Still, he refused to admit to the murders.

Within forty-five minutes, the jury declared Richard Speck guilty. A death sentence was handed down, though, in 1971, it was reduced to life in prison.

At Stateville Correctional Center, Richard would continue to be found with alcohol and drugs until his death from a heart attack on December 5, 1991.

For many, the brutality and randomness of this crime that took the lives of eight people ended the age of innocence in America. These horrors began the horrifying era of seemingly random mass killings. Richard Speck was undoubtedly guilty, but the reason why he chose to kill, methodically and without motive, will never be known.

IV

Janie Lou Gibbs

JANIE LOU GIBBS WAS DESCRIBED BY HER FAMILY, friends, and neighbors as someone who loved children – just loved them to death. So, when her community discovered their beloved church-going housewife's spine-chilling propensities, they were rocked to their core. Janie soon got the names The Georgian Black Widow and The Black Georgian Peach. At the same time, her congregation was left wondering just how many of her donations had been blood money. This is the story of one murderous mother who always made sure to give her ten percent.

A Family Woman

Janie Lou Gibbs (née Hickox) was born on Christmas Day in 1932. She entered the world into a family of seven siblings who lived on a farm in rural Georgia. Her father passed away when she was just four years old, and her mother didn't really fit the profile of a loving or doting parent. She had the difficult task of keeping the farm running and providing for her family all on her own. Janie remembers regularly being assigned chores, most often picking cotton, and never genuinely being close to her mother. However, young Janie was a hard worker and could be found taking care of her siblings when she wasn't tending the crops.

At the tender age of fifteen, Janie met twenty-one-year-old Charles Gibbs, and the pair were soon married. The marriage wasn't one of love but likely more of convenience, as it presented the opportunity of one less mouth to feed for Janie's struggling mother. Nevertheless, the couple stayed together and had three children, remaining married for nearly two decades – until disaster struck.

Janie had always seemed to like children. She helped out with her siblings, worked at a daycare for a time, and even had three boys of her own. Her sons, Robert, Melvin, and Marvin were

55

three years apart. The family settled in Cordell, Georgia, where Janie quickly became a soft-spoken but invaluable member of her community. She occasionally helped with Sunday school at her church and was an active member in religious events and committees. People often described Janie as a kindhearted woman who adored children.

Her other passion was cooking. She often prepared home-cooked meals for her hardworking husband and her three boys. Just as she did on January 21, 1966. Except, the situation was much different this time; the bowl of chili she delivered to her husband in the hospital would be his last.

Charles had been complaining of stomach issues. His health was noted as failing by the owner of the appliance repair company where he worked. In January of 1966, he took a turn for the worst and was admitted to the hospital. On January 21, 1966, he died at only thirty-nine years old. The community gathered around Janie, who appeared to be distraught by his passing after being married to Charles for twenty years.

Janie refused an autopsy, but it was determined from Charles' symptoms it was likely an undiagnosed liver disease that had claimed his life at such a young age.

Her church, in particular, rose up to support the widowed mother; an action that was so appreciated that Janie gave part of her husband's life insurance payout to the religious organization; a generous ten percent contribution.

With the family's supporters rallied around them, Janie and her three boys carried on. Until, just over six months later, severe cramps struck her youngest son, Marvin Jr. Within a few weeks, the thirteen-year-old boy was rapidly deteriorating. On August 29, 1966, he passed away from what doctors speculated was a liver disease inherited from his father. The official cause of death was ruled hepatitis, but Janie again denied an autopsy.

The community of Cordell couldn't believe the terrible tragedy that had befallen Janie, first her husband and then her youngest son. As with Marvin Senior, when the life insurance policy check arrived in the mail, Janie donated a portion of it to the church.

Chilling Coincidences

It seemed likely that two members of the same family could pass from a similar, inherited illness. But neighbors began talking when Janie's middle son, sixteen-year-old Melvin, suddenly started complaining of headaches, dizziness, and cramping. Poor Melvin didn't even make it to the hospital, dying at home after collapsing in the living room on January 23, 1967. Like his brother, doctors diagnosed the teen with hepatitis.

Even if the church was in shock and disbelief at the poor hand Janie had been dealt over the past two years, they still gathered together to come to her aid. Once again, Janie showed her appreciation by donating some of Melvin's life insurance payout to the congregation.

Janie's oldest son was now an only child. However, by the time Melvin passed away, he was married and a father, living in his own home. The community agreed that Melvin's young son must have been a true blessing – a grandson for Janie to dote on in the wake of losing her two boys. The baby appeared to make her happy, or at least he did until his passing. Before he was one month old, the infant died. The town, who had been diligently praying over the baby when he first fell ill, was shocked.

This time, the coincidence was too remarkable for the attending physician. Just a month earlier, Janie's grandson was given a clean bill of health at his birth. An autopsy was ordered, but the findings weren't abnormal. Doctors were baffled, though they wouldn't be for long. Two weeks later, Janie's son, the young new father, started complaining of stomach pain and weakness. Two days after the baffling symptoms appeared, Robert was dead. His autopsy wouldn't be as inconclusive. His liver had severe damage, similar to what doctors had concluded killed his brothers and father. Robert's kidneys were also in a terrible state, especially considering his age and health. Cordell's hospital physicians had now witnessed five members of the Gibbs family, ranging in age from one month to nearly forty, die of liver damage. Testing on the tissues of Robert's body was swiftly ordered.

The test results came back – arsenic poisoning. Fatal levels of arsenic can build up in the body if a person is routinely and unsuspectingly fed small amounts of a common household item, rat poison.

On Christmas Eve 1967, Janie Lou Gibbs was one day shy of thirty-six when she was arrested for the murder of her oldest son. With the incriminating evidence and suspect in hand, investigators ordered the other deceased members of the Gibbs family exhumed.

Autopsies were conducted in the cemetery. Medical examiners laid out the corpses on tarps beside their graves, performing the procedures immediately on-site. The town could not believe that the local daycare owner, loving mother, and doting grandmother was being held on such charges. As Janie's family members were unearthed, her neighbors gathered around the cemetery gates to watch in shocked horror.

Across town, Janie sat in front of investigators. When she was interrogated about the deaths of her sons, husband, and grandson, she replied, "I don't question God's work; the Bible says they will get their just reward, and I'm sure they will."

Every single member of the Gibb family tested positive for arsenic. Police surmised that Janie had slowly and methodically fed her loved one's rat poison until it killed them. She then gave a portion of their life insurance payouts, blood money, to the church. The child-loving, church-going woman was a cold-blooded killer.

Her lawyers believed Janie's only hope was to plead insanity. Though as more details came out, like the fact that Janie delivered the fatal dose of poison via a cup of "get-well-soup" while her husband was in the hospital, attorneys began distancing themselves from the case. Georgia did not have the death penalty at the time. With a shortage of attorneys willing to represent Janie, the court was perplexed about what to do with her. Ultimately, they decided that she was mentally insane and unfit for trial, sentencing her to a mental institution in 1968.

There, Janie spent her days working as one of the cooks for the hospital until 1974. Not even a decade after the murders, a chaplain from the hospital came forward and declared that Janie resolutely knew right from wrong and should have to stand trial for her crimes.

Janie was found guilty of murdering her husband, three sons, and infant grandson – a verdict that earned her five life sentences in prison.

In 1999, Janie was diagnosed with Parkinson's disease. The now sixty-seven-year-old woman was released into the care of her sister, the only family member who had bothered to visit while she was in prison. On February 7, 2010, she passed away in a Georgia nursing home.

Throughout her final years, Janie's sister questioned her motives. Why would she be compelled to kill those she loved dearly her own kin? Janie never could come up with an answer, replying, "I just don't know."

When she died at seventy-seven, Janie had spent almost half her life behind bars. The other half, she used to ruthlessly kill innocent children and her loving husband right under the noses of her caring neighbors and loving church community.

V

Sharon Elizabeth Kinne

S HARON WAS A GIRL WHO ALWAYS WANTED more
in life. More than her rural town, her average life, and the
monotony of a sixty's housewife routine. Unfortunately, she let
her desires get the better of her. While outside observers may have
believed that Sharon just happened to be lucky in various life
circumstances, something much more sinister was happening
behind the scenes.

Lucky in Life?

Sharon Elizabeth Kinne was born Sharon Elizabeth Hall in
1939. Her parents brought her up in their small hometown of

Independence, Missouri. The family briefly lived in Washington State but returned to Independence when Sharon was fifteen. The young girl always hated her rural settings. According to her friends, she never stopped pining for glamorous, big city life. In 1956, at the age of sixteen, Sharon thought she had found her ticket to something better in the form of a young college student named James Kinne.

He was home for the summer from Brigham Young University. The dashing twenty-two-year-old caught Sharon's eye at a church function. He had good looks, but it wasn't about that for Sharon; he had prospects, and she believed he could take her away from Independence. The couple dated for a while in the summer, but then James had to return to school – without Sharon. She had invested months into James and wasn't about to let him slip away, so she wrote him a letter. In it, Sharon informed James of her pregnancy.

James returned home abruptly that same fall, taking a leave from Brigham Young. He promptly married seventeen-year-old Sharon, falsifying the marriage license to say she was an eighteen-year-old widow. Allegedly, Sharon told her friends that she got married while she was in Washington, and her late husband perished in a car crash. However, there were no such records to be found. Nevertheless, the court approved the marriage. James' family gave their blessing as long as Sharon converted to their religion, the Church of Jesus Christ of Latter-Day Saints. James' parents didn't particularly approve of Sharon. Still, the fact that the couple was having a child out of wedlock was shameful enough for the devout Mormon family, and they decided not to make a scene.

Not long after the marriage, Sharon informed James that she had a miscarriage but was still very much invested in the union. Unfortunately, her hopes of moving somewhere glamorous were dashed when James continued his leave from the university and moved with his new bride back to Independence, to a home right next door to his parents. Soon, Sharon was pregnant again with their daughter, Danna. James began working in aviation, and Sharon stayed home to tend to her motherly duties. The family settled down, though Sharon had a penchant for overspending and being over-friendly with other men. Nevertheless, they welcomed another child, a boy, around a year after their daughter.

The marriage began to fall apart when their son was only a few months old. James and Sharon both began to contemplate divorce; however, Sharon told James that she would only give him a divorce if he gave her the house, full custody, and a one thousand dollar alimony check. James strongly suspected Sharon of cheating and admittedly wasn't in the relationship. Still, he did not want to lose custody of their children. Saddened and confused, he went to his parents, who told him to fix the marriage instead of ending it like any good Mormon couple. The pair continued to argue, but James wasn't willing to break up the marriage.

On March 19, 1960, Sharon said she was getting ready for a church dinner in the bathroom while her kids played in the living room and her husband napped in their bedroom. As she bent over the sink to inspect her makeup, she heard her daughter's voice come from the bedroom, "Daddy, how does this thing work?" she asked. Next, she heard a loud bang.

Entering the bedroom, Sharon told police she found two-and-a-half-year-old Danna next to the bed. James lay under the blankets beside a .22 caliber pistol, a bullet hole through the back of his skull. Sharon called the police, but James was pronounced dead, and his death was ruled an accidental shooting. At the scene, police couldn't get much information from a distraught Sharon, and Danna's toddler babbling wasn't of great help either. They decided to spare the two females the sometimes-uncomfortable test of coating the hands in hot paraffin wax to check for gunshot residue.

Investigators didn't fully believe that young Danna could have pulled the trigger. Later, when they called her to the police station and presented her with a similar gun to the one that killed her father, the most she did was turn the safety on and off. Never once did she pull or attempt to pull the trigger. Still, she did have a plethora of cap guns and toy guns and was known to like the loud sound they made when she fired them. Eventually, police had to let their suspicions drop.

When the accidental death was certified, Sharon received a handsome life insurance payment of two hundred fifty thousand dollars. For a grieving wife, Sharon took great joy in spending the check. She also wasted no time in finding a new prospective partner. A visit to the car dealership killed two birds with one stone; she purchased her dream car, a blue Ford Thunderbird, and started a romantic relationship with the car salesman, Walt Jones – despite him being happily married.

Walt's wife, Patricia, worked as a clerk for the IRS during the day and took care of their two kids in the evening and at night. A month into Sharon and Walt's affair, Patricia became suspicious.

Her husband was spending an exorbitant amount of time working late. She couldn't fathom who would be buying a car at eleven at night. Not long after Patricia voiced her fears with her husband, she found out exactly who was occupying her husband's time.

Chilling Coincidences

On Friday, May 27, Walt reported Patricia missing. Walt said the couple had argued Wednesday night, went to bed, and continued not speaking to each other when they parted ways for work Thursday morning. But Thursday night, Patricia never returned home from her job. Walt called his parents and Patricia's co-workers she carpooled with. Her fellow employees told Walt that Patricia had asked them to wait a minute while she went and spoke with a young woman in a Chevy who had pulled into the parking lot. After a brief chat, Patricia returned to her coworkers and asked them to go home without her. As they pulled away, they saw Patricia slip into the seat of the other woman's car. Walt initially suspected Patricia was out with a friend, giving him a taste of his own medicine when it came to working all day and staying out all night. Though, her absence from her children was quite out of character.

Police further questioned the coworkers, and when Walt heard the woman's description, he knew precisely who they were talking about – Sharon. Walt and Sharon had recently gotten into a spat. When he refused to leave his wife, she informed him that she was pregnant. Not believing Sharon's claims, he broke it off with her, returning to his children and his high school sweetheart, Patricia.

Angry, Walt called up Sharon on the phone. She had no hesitation in telling Walt that it was her who had met with Patricia that day. She felt guilty and thought his wife should know of their affair. However, she wasn't entirely forthcoming and had told Patricia that it was her sister that had been sleeping with Walt. Patricia had long suspected Walt of being unfaithful and willingly agreed to meet with Sharon to learn more about her "sister." Sharon told Walt the two women talked until Patricia was about a block away from her house. There, she dropped her off, but not before seeing Patricia talking to a man in a green car, or so she told Walt.

Livid and fearful, Walt went to Sharon's home, demanding to learn his wife's whereabouts. He told police he even went so far as to threaten her with a knife, believing Sharon had done something to get back at him for the breakup. Sharon refused to admit anything, telling him that the last time she saw Patricia was Thursday night while dropping her off at home. At that point, she was alive and well.

Police had barely circulated the missing person's notice when a man showed up at the station around midnight on Friday. His name was John Boldins, and he told police that he had stopped to use the restroom out near a locally known lovers lane hangout when he discovered a body. Authorities quickly went to the scene to investigate, coming upon the corpse of a woman some distance out into an abandoned farm field. Nearby, a purse containing the identification of Patricia Jones was lying haphazardly in the grass. Her body bore bullet holes in her head, shoulders, and abdomen from a .22 pistol fired at close range. Perfectly preserved bullets were still lodged in the soft soil beneath her corpse.

However, a ballistics match wouldn't come as police could not locate the gun. While questioning John Boldizs, the case became more convoluted. What was he doing so far out in the field if he only had stopped to urinate? John claimed that he had actually pulled over his car, and Patricia's dress caught his attention in the headlights. They then asked why he pulled over to begin with. John informed them that he had been on a date and pulled over with a female companion. When they saw the dress, they went to investigate. However, she wanted no involvement with a dead body or the police, and she asked to be dropped off before he reported it.

Naturally, police wanted to follow up with this unidentified female companion. When they pressured him, John finally admitted that he was actively looking for Patricia because his girlfriend had been a friend of the missing woman's who told John that Patricia was probably out parked at the lover's lane with another man to get back at Walt. Not passing up the opportunity to park at seedy hangouts at night with his girlfriend, John readily agreed. That was when they found the bullet-riddled corpse. Police demanded John tell them about his girlfriend, who may have information regarding the death of Patricia. Head in his hands, John gave them her name – Sharon Kinne.

Manipulation and Murder

Of course, police immediately suspected Sharon Kinne, the last person to see Patricia alive. However, the cheating husband, Walt Jones, wasn't in the clear either. Neither was the bumbling yet easily persuaded John Boldizs, Sharon's new boyfriend. All three were interrogated repeatedly. Walt and John passed polygraphs, but Sharon resolutely refused, blaming everything from the death to the discovery on Walt and John.

When investigators searched Sharon's home, they found an empty .22 caliber pistol box. The gun, a replacement that Sharon bought two weeks before the murder of Patricia, was lost not long after she brought it home, she claimed. Police had no forensic evidence to go on but strongly suspected that Sharon might be their killer. The final hope remained with Patricia's corpse and any DNA evidence it might hold.

In another shocking stroke of luck for Sharon, there was a mix-up at the coroner's office. Before the medical examiner could process Patricia's body, a funeral home picked it up. By the time the mistake was realized, and Patricia was returned, her body had already been cleaned and embalmed. Police were no longer able to pinpoint the time of death or get any closer to identifying Patricia's killer.

Nevertheless, on May 31, 1960, police decided to pursue a trial anyway. Not only was Sharon arrested for the murder of Patricia Jones, but also the murder of her late husband, James Kinne.

Sharon had a surprise up her sleeve. As she had done twice before in times of desperation, she told the police that she was pregnant. Only this time, it turned out to be true. However, Sharon was adamant that the child belonged to James Kinne and not Walt Jones. Sharon gave birth in mid-January 1961, likely making the child Walt's.

Six months later, she stood trial for the murder of Patricia. Without a time of death, prosecutors had difficulty pinning the case on Sharon, and the lack of a certified murder weapon also muddied the waters. The jury struggled to grapple with the lack of evidence and the plausible explanations Sharon's costly defense team provided. In the end, she was found not guilty – for Patricia's murder, at least.

Next, Sharon was on the stand for her husband's murder. Believing Patricia's case was the stronger of the two, investigators had placed it before John's. Now, they were worried. In an attempt to gather more evidence, they returned to John Boldizs. At this point, John was married to another woman and had turned on his ex-girlfriend Sharon. He was readily willing to share more, claiming Sharon had once asked him about hiring a hitman to kill James, especially when John turned down her offer of one thousand dollars to kill her husband. This happened two to three weeks before James was found dead. Unfortunately, police believed they needed to get Sharon's confession on tape, a testament that never occurred.

Two years after James Kinne's death, Sharon stood trial for his murder, supported by none other than James' parents. The support was coerced. Sharon's lawyers told the Kinnes' in not so many words that they would need to publicly proclaim their support of Sharon's innocence if they ever wanted to see their grandchildren again.

John Boldizs changed his story too once on the stand, claiming that Sharon's offer to kill her husband was clearly a joke. But the prosecution wouldn't give up and attempted to impeach their own witness due to his dangerous change of heart. Miraculously, the prosecution proved their case to the jury, who found Sharon guilty after nearly six hours of deliberation.

The twenty-two-year-old mother of three received life in prison. Until she appealed, claiming that the prosecution illegally tried to impeach their own witness through improper questioning and identified that the jury pool was, in fact, too small. Sharon only served eighteen months of her life sentence before her appeal was granted. She was released on bail pending another trial.

As March 1964 approached, the date of Sharon's new case, a series of occurrences illustrated the bizarre luck Sharon seemed to possess. First, her initial retrial was declared a mistrial due to a juror selection error; the second retrial in June ended in a hung jury. In October 1964, Sharon was slated to go before the judge for the third time. Only, it wouldn't come to be.

Not because Sharon found some way to get out of it again, but because she was arrested for yet another murder in Mexico.

With her children safely stashed away at her in-law's house, Sharon traveled to Mexico with her new boyfriend, Frank Pugliese. There, she claimed to be Frank's wife, Jeanette Pugliese. Once they crossed the border, they boarded a bus to Mexico City. Whether the couple was there to get married or avoid Sharon's subsequent trial is unknown. What is known is what they did get – extremely ill. After being holed up in their hotel room for days, Sharon decided to leave, allegedly to get medicine. Finding the pharmacy closed, she traveled to the next logical place, a bar. There she met Francisco Paredes Ordonez, a Mexico native who lived in Chicago and had returned for a family visit.

After talking until the wee hours of the morning, the pair went back to Francisco's hotel room. Gunshots rang out at three in the morning, prompting a hotel clerk to enter Francisco's living quarters. Once inside, he found Francisco lying on the bed and Sharon counting money in the bathroom. Startled by the man's entrance, Sharon fired at him. He was struck in the arm but managed to make it out the door, locking it behind him so Sharon couldn't leave.

Sharon Kinne was arrested and charged with murder for the third time. Her attorney supported her self-defense claims, stating Francisco tried to rape her, and the clerk's abrupt entry scared her. Police thought otherwise, as did the media who splashed her moniker, La Pistolera, across papers.

It was leaked that in her hotel room, investigators found a kit full of things to equip someone for life on the run, such as fake identification cards, money, guns, and ammo. One of those guns was of great interest to authorities in Missouri, a .22 caliber pistol. Mexican authorities fired off three rounds from it and mailed the bullets to the police, who were stateside. Ballistics found the bullets from Sharon's gun in Mexico to be an unrefuted match to the ones recovered from beneath Patricia Jones' lifeless body.

Unfortunately, double jeopardy laws prevented Sharon from being retried for Patricia's murder. However, Mexico had no such stipulations. There, she was tried and found guilty, sentenced to ten years. Her appeal was denied and, to make matters worse for Sharon, brought forward the idea that her original sentence was too lenient. Three more years were added to her ten-year sentence.

Upon her release in Mexico, she would be deported to the United States, straight into the hands of waiting police who had grounds to arrest her on her outstanding warrant for missing her October 1967 trial in the case of James Kinne's death.

On December 7, 1969, Sharon had been in prison for five years, learning the language and adapting to societal norms. She watched a movie alone that day while other inmates conversed with their family members for visit day. Suddenly, the jail was plunged into darkness at five in the evening as the building briefly lost power. When the lights flickered on, the warden's set about doing an inmate headcount and roll call. One inmate did not check in – Sharon Kinne.

After Sharon missed a second check-in at two in the morning and was found nowhere on prison grounds, wardens alerted the police to her believed escape. Though the manhunt was extensive, the crafty Sharon had had five years to learn the language, the lay of the land, and the culture. Her nine hour head start made the search nearly impossible.

Sharon Kinne has never been found. It's unknown if the thirty-year-old murderess fled to South America or the United States. The odd coincidences of the power outage, the mysteriously unlocked prison door, and the delayed police alert placed suspicion on the prison guards. However, none admitted to taking a bribe from Sharon or knowing of her escape beforehand. It's more likely that Sharon, as she always seemed to do, got lucky.

VI

Betsy Aardsma

PHYSICALLY, COLLEGE CAMPUSES HAVEN'T changed much over the past fifty to sixty years: large, impressive buildings, stalwarts of the institution tower over grassy lawns where students congregate. Great halls fill with students in rows who take out their textbooks and turn toward the board just as they have for years. And libraries hold towers of dusty books in dimly-lit aisles, fondly referred to as the stacks. A place where some students go to sneak away from prying eyes, a few go to leaf through ancient tomes, and even fewer go to die.

Drive, Determination, and Death

Betsy Aardsma was raised in Holland, Michigan. Brought up as one of four children, the daughter of a tax auditor and a teacher turned stay-at-home mother. The small lakeside town was predominantly Dutch, very religious, and a comfortable place to raise a family.

Active and driven, Betsy did very well for herself both in school and in the community. She was a compassionate child who was regularly involved in community service projects, mission trips, and outreach ventures. Betsy was praised by her teachers as an intelligent student and decided she wanted to be a doctor early on. After graduating, she turned down the University of Michigan to attend Hope College, a nearby Christian school that offered the pre-med track she so desperately desired.

On-campus, Betsy excelled in academics but floundered when finding her place. The curfew and rules were very strict and conservative, while the student body was obedient, if not dull. Additionally, Hope College wasn't the impressive springboard she needed to get into the Peace Corps, her post-graduation dream job. Without looking back, Betsy left the small college after only a few semesters, transferring to the University of Michigan in Ann Arbor in 1967.

During this time, a serial killer known as the Co-ed Killer was running rampant at Eastern University, right next door. However, Betsy took her chances anyway, and they paid off. She fell in love with the liberal college and even switched her major to art and literature. Though the courses were rigorous, Betsey was determined to graduate; and she did. Along with her boyfriend, David Wright, whom she met on campus, the young twenty-year-old was awarded her degree in 1969.

As Betsy once had, David wanted to be a doctor. He was accepted to Penn State's medical program in Hershey, Pennsylvania. Betsy now faced a dilemma, would she continue to be in the Peace Corps currently stationed in Africa post-graduation, or would she give it up for her serious boyfriend? With the promise of something more and the thinly-veiled threat that he wouldn't wait around for her, Betsy decided to pack up her things and move to Pennsylvania with David. Marriage was now the goal she was striving for.

Betsy entered Penn State's English graduate program, which was hosted at a state college, nearly two hours from David's program in Hershey. The couple was serious, but Betsy didn't want to put all her eggs in one basket, occasionally dating other guys until David formally committed. They would see each other when they could but mostly communicated through letters.

Betsy would tell David about her life and her studies throughout the semester. Her letters read like your average correspondence between young sweethearts. However, a letter to her mom depicted a different sentiment: "I don't know why I'm here. I have this weird feeling about being here." Still, by Thanksgiving 1969, Betsy could tell things were heading toward an engagement. She broke off her casual relationships and traveled out to Hershey. After spending the holiday weekend with David and friends, she had to head home to prepare for a looming project. David dropped her off at the bus stop so she could travel back to her campus.

The following day, Friday the 28th, Betsy set out in the early afternoon to meet with two professors and finally take care of some research at the Pattee Library. That night she had planned to meet her friend and roommate, Sharon Brandt, for a movie.

On level three, Betsy stopped to peruse the card catalog for the reference location of the book she needed. It was on the second floor, aisle 51. The stacks of Penn State often gave Betsy the creeps, with their "low ceilings, dim light, and narrow staircases." She slowly made her way down the aisle, her red knit dress brushing the worn spines of the book. At last, she made her way to the core, the center of the stacks, glancing up briefly when Dean Brungart passed by. When another student, Shirley Brooks, obscured by shadows, approached Betsy asking for a pen, she nearly jumped out of her skin. Upon Shirley's return of the pen, Betsy asked her the time; it was fifteen minutes before five in the afternoon came the response.

Shirley would be the last person to see Betsy alive.

A Slaying in the Stacks

Richard Allen forced the paper into the agonizingly slow copy machine on level two of the stacks. The hushed conversation he heard nearby only added to the macabre of the place, like ghosts whispering through the dusty aisles. Suddenly, the sound of heavy books falling to the floor shattered the quiet, followed by a loud metal clang.

Glancing up from the copier, a man running out of aisle 51 caused him to do a double-take. Staring at the quickly moving figure in shock, David was even more surprised when the man yelled, "That girl needs help!" Then he briskly made his way down the staircase. Another student followed behind, believing that the first man was going to get help and he would assist him. When the second student returned, stating that the man who called for help outran him, Marilee Erdley, the front desk attendant, hustled to aisle 51 to see what the commotion was about.

There, she saw Betsy lying on the floor, her upper body propped slightly upright against the lower shelves. A small puddle of liquid lay between haphazardly fallen volumes. It appeared that the young girl had fainted. After Marilee couldn't bring Betsy around, she summoned the paramedics and called the janitorial staff to clean up the puddle that she surmised was urine. While waiting, Marilee and another student, Joao Uafinda, began cleaning up the dropped books.

When the medical team arrived, they placed Betsy on a stretcher and took her to the campus medical center. There, it was noted that Betsy wasn't breathing. Fearing a stroke or something more serious, they immediately started chest compressions; within the first few downward thrusts, a sticky, wet liquid bloomed from Betsy's chest. The doctor removed her red-knit dress to find a clean and clearly deep puncture wound. An autopsy later revealed that a knife had plunged three inches directly into her heart.

The stab was precise and forceful, severing her pulmonary artery and piercing the right ventricle. She had bled very little on the surface, as all the blood had pooled inside her body, rapidly filling her lungs. What little did ooze from the wound was masked by Betsy's red knit dress. Dr. Thomas Magnani declared her time of death as nineteen minutes after five. However, she likely passed away just minutes after the stabbing, which he noted was an intentional aim for the heart by a right-handed assailant. The medical response team's stomachs lurched as they quickly realized they went from responding to a fainting woman to finding a murder victim who had just been declared dead.

Back at the library, the murder scene had been wiped clean. The books were restored to their proper places, the floor was mopped, and the student witnesses had dispersed, believing a girl had fainted. The paramedics had safely taken her to the campus medical center to regain her senses.

Police had no evidence and a handful of unknown witnesses that could be any of the hundreds of students at the university.

The first order of business was to find the students who had been present for Betsy's murder and interview her close contacts. Thirty-five state troopers combed the campus, working from their home base in the Boucke Building. After they rounded up the few students who had unknowingly been party to a murder, they discovered that the man barreling out of the stacks where Betsy was slain was around six feet tall, one-hundred-eighty-five pounds, with brown hair and glasses, and a young age that likely meant he was a student. Not only were they looking for the killer, but also his murder weapon, believed to be a three-and-a-half to four-inch hunting knife.

The cleanup of the crime scene further hindered their progress, leaving only three drops of blood on the nearby staircase. Richard Allen reported the conversation he heard was not aggressive or harsh but casual and calm. Police surmised that Betsy knew her killer and felt comfortable around him. Despite hundreds of students and staff being interviewed, polygraphs being administered, and a twenty-five thousand dollar reward being offered, the authorities search produced no leads.

Her boyfriend, David Wright, was miles away, had an alibi, and no motivation to kill his girlfriend. He was quickly eliminated as a suspect. After days of exhaustive interviewing and searching, police were no closer to finding the murderer who lurked in the library.

Theories Abound

Many campus residents developed their own theories about who could have killed Betsy Aardsma. Some speculated that she stumbled upon nefarious activities. A few students put forth a drug deal. In contrast, others suggested a secret homosexual relationship as the persons engaged would face serious professional and personal disaster if found out. This suggestion generated some interest from the police when more than twenty pornographic magazines were discovered tucked between the books near the spot where Betsy was murdered. Fingerprints collected from the magazine did not produce a match in the police database.

Police grappled with the question of whether the murder was preplanned or random. Betsy seemed to know her killer, and his meticulous stab of the blade didn't allow her to call out as she slipped silently to the floor. However, who would've known where to find Betsy, or precisely when she would have been in the stacks? Her activities that afternoon weren't routine, and she didn't discuss her plans with anyone.

Despite this, by Christmas 1969, the police had narrowed their suspect list down to two – Richard Haefner and William Spencer.

William Spencer actually put himself on authorities' radar. The forty-year-old sculptor was a campus regular, as his wife was there studying for her doctorate, and he found a job in the art department. At a holiday faculty party, Spencer claimed that he was the one who "killed that girl in the library." He had known her because she was a nude model in the art department. He later recanted this statement, and authorities discovered that conservative Betsy was never a nude model.

Police followed up with Spencer, who informed them during an interview that he had seen someone jogging away from the library and could sculpt a bust of their perpetrator. However, his descriptions of the killer were wildly inaccurate compared to the first-hand accounts of the witnesses who were in the library. Spencer's wife confided in the police that they should entirely ignore her husband, which they did after Spencer proved to know nothing of the case.

Next was Richard Haefner, a fellow student who had a history of abuse toward women, child molestation, and obsessive behavior; he once followed a girl he was interested in eight hundred miles back to her hometown only to show up on her doorstep unexpectedly. She had to threaten him with the police before he left. However, Richard was interested in men and went on dates with women only to keep up appearances. One of these women was Betsy Aardsma.

After Richard faced accusations of theft from the geology department where he studied, he had a bit of a breakdown. These mental health episodes allegedly led to Betsy breaking off their friendship. He lived directly across the courtyard that students had to pass through to access the library. His appearance also fit the suspect's profile, having brown hair and frequently seen wearing khakis, glasses, and a sports coat. Haefner maintained that he had never set foot in the library and was eating dinner in the students' Union building at the time of the killing. While no one could corroborate this, one professor said that shortly after the murder, Haefner bounded up his steps and knocked on his door, shouting in a giddy and excited manner, "Did you hear that my ex-girlfriend has just been killed?!"

Police had no evidence against Haefner and were forced to let the case go cold.

On the 25th anniversary of her death, in 1994, someone left a lit candle in the aisle where Betsy had been killed, even though all the aisles had been renumbered by this time. Beside the candle, written directly on the floor in red marker, was a message reading: "RIP Betsy Aardsma, born July 11th, 1947, died November 28th, 1969. I am back." Accompanying the chilling message were clippings from newspapers circa 1969 detailing the events of her death and the ensuing investigation. Police eventually declared that it was an ill-conceived prank.

Then, in 2009, Haefner's nephew came forward, recalling a 1975 conversation between Haefner and his mother that he had overheard. In it, Haefner's mother allegedly admonished Richard for arousing police suspicion regarding that he "killed that girl" after "all [her] efforts" to protect him. Finishing off the conversation with a damning "You killed that girl, and now you're killing me!"

In an ironic twist of fate, Richard Haefner died from a torn aorta in 2002. Blood instantaneously filled his lungs just as it had Betsy's.

VII

Peyton-Allan Murders

LARRY PEYTON AND BEVERLY ALLAN SEEMED TO have everything going for them in the summer of 1960. The teens both found a seasonal job at Crater Lake National Park in southern Oregon. The breathtaking Cascade Mountains were the perfect backdrop for their breakneck romance. As luck would have it, both Larry and Beverly lived and went to school on the west coast, even if a five-hour drive separated them. It would be on one of these weekend trips that the couple's good luck would run out – entirely.

Star-Crossed Lovers

Larry Peyton's father owned a motor lodge right outside Crater Lake National Park. Larry had long spent his summers working there, as he did during the warm months of 1960 while on break from Portland State College. However, that summer season would be different from the rest. Larry's life changed as soon as he was introduced to his colleague, Beverly Ann Allan. She was born and raised in Port Townsend, Washington, but had come to Crater Lake for a summer job. She took courses at Western Washington University, a five-hour drive from Larry's institution.

Though they were only nineteen and newly introduced, their romance heated up quickly. By the end of the summer, they were dating. By mid-fall, they were in a committed relationship, and after spending the Thanksgiving holiday with one another, they were discussing marriage.

After seeing her parents in Port Townsend, Washington, Beverly drove to Portland to spend the long weekend with Larry. They met up with friends, had dinner, and decided to go shopping at the Lloyd Center the Friday after Thanksgiving, November 26, 1960. It was around nine at night before the pair departed Larry's home. Around ten thirty, they joined some friends in downtown Portland before the group parted ways, and Larry and Beverly went on to enjoy each other's company.

Teens, especially those in love, were apt to stay out late, but Larry's parents became worried when the two weren't back by the following morning. They hurriedly contacted the police and filed missing person's reports for both, as Beverly was last seen with Larry and they had both failed to return home. This wasn't a regular occurrence for either of the well-mannered and bright college students.

On November 27th, Portland police were going about their usual rounds, hitting all the local teenage hangouts. One such place was a well-known lover's lane. The remote spot, obscured by trees, was on Portland's northwest side in an area known as Forest Park. Five hundred yards off the road, the secluded nook was regularly swept by authorities. However, what was uncommon was the discovery police would make on that fateful day.

A car sat wedged up an embankment, an awkward angle for two teens seeking privacy. Even more peculiar was that the driver's side door was flung open to the chilly fall evening air. The officers exited their patrol car and approached the vehicle. Their flashlight beam swept the interior of the Ford coupe before falling on a grim shape hunched over the steering wheel. Further investigation found that the form belonged to a young man whose body showed signs of blunt force trauma to the head and stab wounds.

The vehicle's inside was splattered with blood, illustrating that he had not gone down without a fight. It leaked from the open door and pooled under the car. In front of the cold, curled-up corpse was a single bullet hole through the windshield of the coupe, and on the hood was a small penknife. Evidence of another person in the car, a female, made the discovery even more gruesome. Inside was a woman's coat, purse, a scrap of a ripped blouse, and a piece of a torn fingernail. The woman was nowhere to be found.

Police had found one of their missing persons. The body was positively identified as Larry Peyton, and the purse belonged to Beverley Allan. With haste, the first officers who discovered the murder began looking for clues. They gained valuable insight, such as three dollars in Larry's wallet and eleven dollars in Beverly's purse, which led them to believe robbery was not the motive. Nearby they found Larry's car keys as if the killer had tossed them, thwarting any chances of escape. Beverly's glasses and a length of nylon rope were found outside the vehicle.

However, the clue-hungry police also destroyed vital evidence, including fingerprints, which would make the case challenging to solve.

An autopsy of Larry found that he had a skull fracture from a blunt object, believed to be the butt of a gun. It wasn't bullets that riddled the front and back of his torso but stab wounds, twenty-three of them from a four-inch blade. None of them matched the penknife found on the hood of Larry's coupe. The bullet hole in the windshield was the result of a gun being discharged from inside the car.

Beverly's whereabouts were still unknown and the police operated under the assumption that she had been abducted when her boyfriend had been murdered.

On the Hunt for the Lover's Lane Killer

Dogs scoured the lover's lane area and nearby. They could only track Beverly's scent for half a mile from the car. Further away, the dogs picked it up once more but lost it quickly, telling police Beverly had been taken from the scene in a vehicle.

Christmas approached, and the police still had no answers. No one in the community possessed any ill will toward the young couple. They had gone to a well-known, if secluded, hangout with no witnesses. It was unknown if Beverley was alive or dead, killed by the same hands as Larry's mystery murderer. Or murderers. Police began suspecting that two people had attacked the couple, one armed with a gun and the other with a knife; both were likely men.

As Larry and Beverly's spaces sat empty at family Christmas, televisions and newspapers displayed their faces, keeping the case at the forefront of everyone's mind. Beverly's father added a one-thousand-dollar reward to the newspaper articles and reports, but no one came forward.

Just after the holiday, a chilling message was found on a bathroom mirror; written in red lipstick, it read: "Help Me." But police quickly dismissed it as fake due to the fact that two lipsticks were found in Beverly's purse in the car, making it unlikely she would be carrying a third on her person.

Forty-four days after the discovery of Larry, on January 9, 1961, Beverly was recovered – beaten and battered, ice-cold, and very much dead. Propped up against a few saplings that had prevented her from falling down a nearby ravine, her body lay on US Highway 26, thirty miles northwest of Portland. A road worker had noticed her peculiar form against the bleak, snowy landscape. However, she was far from the roadside, making it possible she could have been in this spot for six weeks or more.

She was partially clothed, missing a shoe, and face down. Nearby, her ski sweater lay haphazardly. She was bound with a nylon cord, matching the sample taken from the scene. The cold January weather made it particularly hard to determine Beverly's cause and time of death. An autopsy did reveal that she had been sexually assaulted and strangled. Still, it was unknown if she was strangled manually or with a rope.

Ultimately, the coroner believed that she had been murdered on November 27. But rumors that she had been kept alive for weeks after being abducted abounded.

Despite interviewing over two thousand two hundred ninety-two witnesses, following leads about cars that had been stopped nearby, and spending two hundred fifty thousand dollars on search efforts, there were four hundred and fifty-three suspects police eventually cleared or didn't pursue further. After one year of investigation, the case file was two thousand and twenty pages long.

One of those suspects was Edward W. Edwards. By the time police stumbled upon him as a person of interest, he was in jail for making a false call to the fire department. But his unexplained bullet wound was suspicious. He escaped before they arranged a time to interview him in the Portland jail, eventually being placed on the FBI's most-wanted list.

In 1962, he was captured in Cleveland, and at that time, he gave a reasonable explanation for his bullet wound. Police stopped looking into Edwards as the killer.

In June 1965, police decided to exhume Beverly's body from her hometown cemetery in Port Townsend. They wanted to re-examine her time of death. The second round of testing finally put the rumors of her being held against her will for an extended period to rest; it was determined that she died shortly after being taken from the car. However, with this final piece of evidence, the case went cold.

The Jorgensens

In 1966, after giving an interview to a reporter, police received a letter from Veronica Essex, who went by Niki. She said that she had information to share with detectives concerning the murders of Larry and Beverly.

After speaking with her, she gave police several pieces of the story that weren't leaked to the media, making her report credible in their eyes as only someone who had witnessed the crime firsthand would be knowledgeable about these details. Nikki claimed that three men, in particular, were involved, Carl Jorgensen, Eddie Jorgensen, and Robert Brom.

The police showed up at Mr. and Mrs. Jorgensen's home, only to find their seven children had all since grown up and left. Two of those children were Eddie and Carl. The Jorgensens' recalled their sons being at a house party in the West Hills near the murder on that fateful night but denied that either could have any involvement in such a heinous act.

On August 19, 1968, bolstered by the testimony of other witnesses along with Nikki, police set out to arrest Carl Jorgensen, Eddie Jorgensen, and their friend Robert Gordon Brom. Edward, the owner of an automotive garage, was arrested in bed in his home as his wife and children looked on. Carl was apprehended when he walked into his job at a high-end shoe store. Robert Brom turned out to be in Portland, not Salem as they had thought, and was picked up later that afternoon. He was on parole at the time of his apprehension for previously assaulting a grocery store clerk.

They were all charged with two counts of first-degree murder and appeared in court in September. Separately, over the course of two months, they were charged. Eyewitnesses and the testimony of Nikki placed the three at the scene and detailed their interactions with the deceased.

Nikki said that the brothers and Brom met up with Larry and Beverly on Friday, November 26, 1960, at a local restaurant. From there, Nikki persuaded the young lovers to join them at the West Hills house party. On the way, the two cars, one driven by Larry and the other by one of the Jorgensens, began racing, nearly crashing at one point. The Jorgensens' vehicle suffered damages, forcing them to trade out their car for someone else's they picked up on the way to the party. It was then they met up with Larry again, but this time they weren't so friendly. They were angered over the accident and the resulting damage to their car, so they initiated a car chase.

The chase ended off a dead-end road in Forest Park. There, the three men got out of the car and approached Larry while

Nikki waited in the vehicle. She heard the fight ensue but said she didn't witness the murder. Not long after, the men returned with Beverly in tow. Together, they headed to Nikki's home, where Brom dropped her off, and all three left with Beverly.

Nikki testified that she didn't come forward sooner because she had repressed the trauma as a young eighteen-year-old; it was only with hypnosis and truth serum that she was able to recall what she had seen, now in her mid-twenties. Other witnesses corroborated her statement – including Lorraine Jorgensen (unrelated to the brothers). Lorraine claimed that in a drunken state, both Edward and Carl had once told her about the details of the murder.

Despite the defense repeatedly claiming that Nikki and Lorraine were not of sound mind and had no physical evidence, the two men were charged with murder. Edward received the second-degree murder of Larry and the first-degree murder of Beverly. Robert was charged with the first-degree murder of Larry. Carl was acquitted. Both men charged were handed down a sentence of life plus twenty-five years, and unsurprisingly, they both appealed.

After a very short prison stint, Edward and Robert would walk free. Not because of their appeals, which were denied, but because they were both paroled. Edward only served three years and Robert, even with his prior violent convictions, served only seven years.

Some still believe that Robert and Edward were not guilty all along, citing their early parole as the police trying to right a wrong. They claim that it was actually Edward W. Edwards, which may hold water. Edward W. Edwards was, after all, discovered near the scene of the crime with a mysterious bullet wound. Even though he gave an explanation upon his arrest after escaping, he would later be charged with the murders of two couples, one in Wisconsin and one in Ohio.

Both murders were similar to the killing of Larry and Beverly. Edward W. Edwards is a person of interest in many lover's lane killings from the fifties and sixties, and some speculate that he could be the Zodiac Killer.

He died in prison in 2011, never confirming or denying his role in the brutal slayings of the young teenagers in love, Larry Peyton and Beverly Allan.

VIII

Graeme Thorne

TODAY, THE SYDNEY OPERA HOUSE IS synonymous with Australia. However, in 1960 it was still being built. The government of New South Wales decided that lotteries would be an excellent way to generate funds for the increasingly expensive construction of the enormous building. Winning the first prize of A£100,000 (around A$3.1 million) would seem like a dream come true, but it quickly devolved into a nightmare for the Thorne family.

The Thorne Family

Bazil Thorne and his family rented a house in a small town named Bondi. Nearly three hundred miles from Sydney, it was to be the home of the brand-new Opera House. The construction of the monolithic building was initially expected to cost seven million pounds and take four years to build. However, the New South Wales government quickly realized that these numbers were far too modest. It would cost considerably more to erect their new monument to the arts, closer to one hundred million pounds, in fact. So, with various failed fundraising efforts under their belts, they decided on one last attempt to drum up money. They would hold a lottery.

The winnings from these state government lotteries were around one hundred thousand pounds for the cost of a three-pound ticket, no small sum, to be sure. Winners were a big deal and always had their faces splashed across the newspapers and reporters waiting to track their every move.

Bazil Thorne bought the occasional ticket here and there but had only ever had modest winnings. As a traveling salesman, in partnership with his father, he was often on the road. He visited the gas stations where tickets were typically sold. He hated to leave his wife Freda, their three-year-old daughter Belinda, and their eight-year-old son Graeme at home, but there was no way around life on the road. Graeme's education at The Scots College in Bellevue Hill wasn't cheap; plus, his eldest daughter Cheryl was institutionalized for life with permanent disabilities.

It was in Gunnedah, as Bazil was writing up orders for the store, when Bazil began contemplating purchasing another ticket. However, before he could withdraw his wallet, the telephone rang, and the person on the other end was asking for him. A newspaper reporter informed him that he had just won the latest Opera House lottery drawing. Bazil didn't believe it at first, but when the caller read out the winning numbers, Bazil confirmed they matched his. His face went pale, and he struggled to stand. The payout? One hundred thousand pounds or two point eight million today.

Bazil quickly flew home. Upon arriving in Sydney on Wednesday, June 1, 1960, he was greeted by a bevy of reporters wanting to know what he would do with his newfound wealth. The reserved Bazil told reporters that he wouldn't be reckless and would likely put the money into savings until he and his wife could figure out what to do with it all, telling the men, "I believe the saying charity begins in the home, and I intend to make this my policy." After all, his business partner was his aging father, who he didn't want to leave high and dry. Cheryl also needed year-round care, which cost money. His greatest aspiration at the time was to hopefully stop renting and buy a home for him, Freda, Belinda, and Graeme.

It was no surprise that the next day the papers read: "100,000-pound win – too young to retire." Accompanied by a photo of thirty-seven-year-old Bazil Thorne and as was customary at the time, the Thornes' home address.

Three-Quarters of a Million Dollars

At 79 Edward Street, life carried on as usual in the Thorne household, despite their burgeoning bank account. Bazil still traveled, Freda took care of Belinda at home, and Graeme went off to school each morning. He would wait at the intersection of Wellington and O'Brien streets, not even a quarter of a mile from his home. At this corner was also a small market, which Graeme frequented each morning to buy a bag of chips and talk to the shop owner.

It was like clockwork. Graeme kissed his mother goodbye at eight-thirty, walked to the corner, bought a bag of chips, and talked to the man behind the counter until a few minutes before nine in the morning when Phyllis Smith, a family friend whose sons attended the same school, would pick him up in her car.

But on the hot and humid morning of July 7, Graeme was nowhere to be seen when Phyllis pulled up. Scanning the nearly empty corner and not finding the young boy, she pulled alongside the curb and decided to get out. Entering the store, she asked the manager if he had seen Graeme. The man remarked that he thought it was odd the boy wasn't there this morning. No one wearing the traditional school uniform of a gray sweater and shorts and carrying a sixteen-inch bookcase emblazoned with the student's name in the corner, was anywhere in sight.

Initially, Phyllis thought maybe Graeme had gone to school without her, but a search conducted by the headmaster proved otherwise. Next, Phyllis figured perhaps he was running late, so she decided to drive to the Thorne home just to be sure. Freda was deeply unsettled to find that Graeme was not at school or with Phyllis. She immediately called the police on her newly connected phone line.

When a deputy and sergeant arrived, Freda diligently described her missing eight-and-a-half-year-old son. The deputy took notes and assured Freda they would begin looking for her child. Before he could leave the Thornes' household, the phone rang. The male caller asked, "Is that you, Mrs. Thorne?" He then inquired after Bazil, who was on the road.

When Freda asked why he was looking for Bazil, the man responded, "I have your son." Nearby, the sergeant could tell something had shifted in Freda's demeanor, and he motioned for her to hand him the phone. As soon as he was on the line, the foreign, male voice spoke: "I have your boy; I want 25,000 pounds before 5 o'clock this afternoon; I'm not fooling; if I don't have the money by 5, I will feed the boy to the sharks. I'll phone back at 5 with instructions."

At first, the police were perplexed; twenty-five thousand pounds was equivalent to nearly three-quarters of a million pounds today. When Freda explained their recent lottery win, the police began their manhunt in earnest.

Australia had never before dealt with a child kidnapping for ransom. Their search would become the biggest in New South Wales history. Bazil Thorne was summoned to the airport desk as soon as he touched down in Sydney. The police told him about Graeme's disappearance. Still, he didn't know about the ransom until he reunited with Freda at home. All day, police knocked on every door in the area, each occupant claiming they hadn't seen anything unusual.

Police suspected a group of people, including a woman, had intercepted Graeme and were responsible for the kidnapping. The caller's accent and the fact that kidnappings were unheard of in Australia led authorities to believe that the kidnappers were foreign and had recently arrived in the country. Freda and Bazil said they would do whatever it took, pay whatever amount, to get their son back.

Everyone sat by the phone, the room silent with tension, but five o'clock passed, and the kidnapper never called. Freda was in such a state that she had to be sedated; Bazil refused to sleep and sat by the telephone all night. Police found that an unlisted number made the first call, but they could not identify where it had originated from. Finally, at a quarter to ten, the phone rang again. An officer intercepted the call, pretending to be Bazil and attempting to stall the caller so a trace could be performed. The man on the other end explained how the exchange would happen; two paper bags full of money were to be left – but the line went dead before the man could tell the Thornes' where the drop was to occur.

Police questioned neighbors, showed photos and plastered his picture across television screens. Bazil and the police gave public pleas and statements. All officers on leave were called back, and vacations and leaves were eliminated over the course of the search. Every police station in New South Wales was alerted and on the lookout. Twenty-four-hour surveillance of the Thornes' home was instated. But police could still not figure out how the kidnapper had the Thornes' phone number, which was only recently installed and unlisted. Then Freda explained an odd occurrence that she hadn't thought anything of – until now.

In May, they received a telephone line, but it took months to be connected. When the line still remained unconnected in mid-June, a man stopped by their home. Usually, reporters who wanted to interview them would simply knock on their door. It was commonplace for the Thornes'. However, this man was different. He claimed to be a private investigator and stated he was looking for a man named Bognor. They tried to direct him to an upstairs neighbor who had lived on the premises for decades, but he would not be dissuaded. At one point, he asked them if a phone number he had written in his notebook was theirs. Shocked, the Thornes' replied that, yes, that was their number, though their phone line had yet to be connected. The "private investigator" assured them he had means of finding their unconnected and unlisted number. He then left, and the Thornes' chalked up the unnerving experience to a mistake.

Police published an appeal in three different languages, German, Italian, and Greek, across all the Sydney papers. They urged citizens to be on the lookout, rewards were offered, interceptions were set up at all major roads and ports, and the government even offered a free pardon to any accomplice if the kidnapper let Graeme go free and an arrest was made. Hardened criminals associated with Sydney's underworld stepped forward to help the police, as no one took kindly to the kidnapping of a child.

Neighbors searched their yards, and authorities scoured every waterway, road, and plot of land. Finally, a tip came in. A dark-colored car had been spotted not long after Graeme's disappearance. It pulled into a gas station twenty miles west of the Thornes'. A group occupied the vehicle, consisting of two men, a woman, and a boy matching Graeme's description. They asked for fuel and then left, the owner taking down their rear license plate number as the car disappeared into the night. The next day, Friday, July 8, when an off-duty officer spotted the vehicle and approached, it sped off. A high-speed chase ensued, but the car was lost in heavy traffic. Its number plates weren't registered to a vehicle matching its description.

In Parkland, around thirteen miles north of the site of Graeme's disappearance, a seventy-five-year-old resident was walking around an area of abandoned land, just off a major road, not far from the gas station where the car was spotted. As the man bent to collect bottles from some dense undergrowth, he spotted a schoolboy's leather briefcase with the initials G. Thorne on the lower corner. It was empty inside. He hid the case under a large rock and told his son-in-law later that evening, who promptly informed the authorities. Once the case was retrieved, his parents confirmed it was his, but no more leads turned up in the area. Detectives thought it might have been tossed from a moving car.

The next clue would come when police again questioned Freda about the man who claimed to be a private investigator. Neighbors had described seeing a similar man sitting across from the Thornes' home for weeks, seated on a park bench, always with a newspaper across his face. Just after eight in the morning on the day of Graeme's disappearance, the same man was seen double-parked in an iridescent blue 1955 Ford Customline at the intersection where Phyllis typically picked up Graeme.

112

A Kidnapper Turned Killer

On Sunday, July 10, one mile north of the discovery of Graeme's briefcase, the boy's clothing was found. The police instantly recognized it as planted. That area had been continually patrolled. The items were perfectly dry, even though a steady rain had fallen the night before. Officers recovered a Scout's college schoolboy cap, a torn paper with Graeme's handwriting, a wrapped apple prepared just as Freda had always done for Graeme, a textbook, and a raincoat draped over a small kerosene drum. Unfortunately, none of these clues indicated where Graeme could be.

On August 16, 1960, it had been six weeks since Graeme disappeared. A few children were playing near a treehouse they had erected on the edge of a vacant plot of land. Nearby, a previously unseen carpet roll, tied with rope, looked as if it had been dumped and abandoned. One of the boys described the carpet to his father that evening. Along with a neighbor, the man decided to take a closer look. Armed with flashlights, they cut the bindings of the rug. Peeling back one of the corners, the man saw what appeared to be hair. Throwing off the rest of the rug, a small form was uncovered, unmistakably human, although partially decomposed. A scarf was around the boy's neck, and rope bound his ankles and wrists.

Police immediately flooded the scene. Graeme's body had a skull fracture caused by blunt force trauma; he had strangulation marks around his neck. The cause of death was either blunt force trauma or asphyxia. Due to the advanced decomposition, he was suspected of having been killed shortly after being abducted, no more than twenty-four hours after being grabbed off the street. His clothes were precisely as they were when he had left the Thorne home, his coat fully buttoned and his handkerchiefs neatly folded and unused in his pockets. Fungus on his shoes proved that he had been killed, rolled in the rug, and abandoned for nearly six weeks.

Looking closely at the rug, they discovered the date of production and the plant at which it was manufactured. Its woolen check design was broadcast to the public, asking anyone to report having seen a similar rug before. Both animal and human hairs were found embedded in the carpet and on the scarf around Graeme's neck. Plant matter was also uncovered, belonging to soil and foliage that did not naturally occur in or near where the body was found. Pink mortar dust coated the back of his coat, alluding to the fact that he was likely kept under a brick building after being killed.

The young boy's service was heavily attended by some five hundred people. The manhunt for the murderer only intensified.

Police were on the lookout for a brick home that matched the pink mortar, a blue 1955 Ford Customline, and two of the particular trees that matched the foreign plant matter found on the body. A postman would tip off the authorities, directing them to 28 Moore Street in the suburb of Clontarf, just a mile from where Graeme's corpse was discovered. The home was owned by a Hungarian immigrant named Stephen Bradley, whose build and features matched the description of the man police had been hunting for. The family even owned a Pekingese as a pet.

Yet he was friendly and helpful, telling officers that he had been home all day on the morning of Graeme's kidnapping, and his car had never left the garage. Thirty-four-year-old Bradley had been married three times, one of his former wives dying under suspicious circumstances. With his third wife, he had fraud charges placed against him, and the couple suffered a mysterious fire in their home. A series of insurance claim profits brought them to their well-to-do home in Sydney in 1959. However, they quickly ran out of funds to provide for their three children and the lavish lifestyle they had become accustomed to.

The day after Bradley was interviewed, his wife booked a ship ticket to London for herself and a son. Bradley followed suit, purchasing passages for himself and their other two children. One month later, they were gone – selling all their worldly belongings, cutting ties with everyone in Australia, and telling no one. They simply disappeared.

Bradley disembarked in Columbo, Sri Lanka, leaving his wife and children aboard. Police were unaware that he had fled the country.

In October 1960, the Thornes' identified Steven Bradley's photo in a lineup as the private investigator who had knocked on their door. Furthermore, rug fibers matching the carpet that held Graeme's body were found at the Bradley's abandoned home. On October 17th, police brought the case against Bradley, who they now knew was on the run. They planned to extradite him from Sri Lanka.

Bradley was extradited to Australia on November 18, 1960. Bradley, who initially claimed he was innocent, signed a confession upon his arrival in Sydney, writing: "I went out and watched the Thorne boy leaving the house and seen him for about three mornings, and I have seen where he went. And one morning, I have followed him to the school at Bellevue Hill. One or two mornings I have seen a womman [sic] pick him up, and take him to the school. On the day we moved from Clontarf I went out to Edward Street. I parked the car in a street I don't know the name of the street it is off Wellington Street. I have got out from the car, and I waited on the cornor [sic], until [sic] the boy walked down to the car. Then the boy got in the car...I asked for 25,000 from the boys [sic] mother and father. I took the boy home in the car. I told him to get out of the car. When he got out of the car, I put a scarf around his neck and put him in the boot of the car and slammed the boot." Bradley claimed he left Graeme there until it was dark that evening, at which point he opened the trunk to find the young boy dead.

In court, he pled guilty to kidnapping but not guilty to murder, stating his confession was forced. Forensics disproved his initial admission, illustrating that a person could breathe air in the trunk for seven hours. What's more, they showed a picture of Bradley's wife wearing a scarf of the same style and design as the one that had been tied around Graeme's neck. The jury needed only three hours and twenty-two minutes to find Bradley guilty.

The crowd in the courtroom clapped and cheered; Freda wept.

Bradley said, "I knew before I came to this court, I would be convicted of a crime I did not commit." He cited prejudice as the main factor of the jury's decision, claiming the case's publicity put him at an unfair disadvantage from the beginning.

Steven Bradley was sentenced to penal servitude for life at Goulburn jail. His wife divorced him, and he had to live a life separated from other prisoners, dying at age forty-two from a heart attack in 1968.

The addresses of lottery winners were never again printed in the papers without consent.

IX

Christine Rothschild

CAMPUS CRIMES RARELY GO UNNOTICED BUT are often downplayed or swept under the rug entirely. Such was the case with the forgotten campus murder of Christine Rothschild. Universities and colleges stand to lose a great deal when one of their students is ruthlessly murdered. No one feels safe, often resulting in parents flocking to the campus to retrieve their terror-stricken teenagers. But then, the media moves on, people forget, and college life slowly resumes as if nothing ever happened.

A Brilliant and Beautiful Student

Christine Rothschild was known to all her friends as "Chris." In the spring of 1967, she graduated from Senn High School in Chicago, Illinois. She had been raised there by her family, consisting of her two parents and six siblings – three of whom lived past childhood. Her father was a hard worker and was able to afford an upscale two-story home in the posh suburbs of Chicago. Both the Rothschild daughters were raised to be proper, prim, and capable of making excellent wives. They were taught etiquette by their socialite mother, who hoped for nothing more than a solid marriage for each of her daughters. However, Christine's father taught her to dream and aspire to more. By the time she graduated, she was opinionated, independent, and adored by many of her classmates.

Blonde and quite breathtaking, the petite Christine worked as a model for Saks Fifth Avenue the summer before and after graduating. She was as brilliant as she was beautiful, ranking fourth out of a class of five hundred. A well-rounded woman who was bright and hardworking, Christine wanted to attend Vassar College in Poughkeepsie, New York. Still, her parents urged her to go to Madison's University of Wisconsin, especially her mother, who wanted to keep her close to home.

Ultimately, Christine acquiesced to her mother's wishes and went to the University of Wisconsin. It was just far enough away that she could have a taste of freedom. In the fall of 1967, her parents dropped her off at Ann Emery Hall, an on-campus dormitory. There, she was one of one hundred eighty-eight girls living in student housing. Linda Tomaszewski Shulko was one of these other girls. She lived in another dormitory but happened to run into Christine a few times during the first few weeks of school. They became fast friends. The girls were very close and often attended campus events together, such as sports and plays. Self-described as nerds, they were serious about academia. Christine wanted to be a national affairs journalist. As such, they rarely went to parties or bars, preferring to study.

As the girls became closer, Linda discovered that Christine was serious about something other than school – her weight. She only ever drank coffee, smoked cigarettes, and ate canned spinach, at times taking laxatives if she ever veered from her diet. She always brushed it off when Linda asked, and, smitten with her friend and how like-minded they were, Linda never pushed. The girls abhorred fraternity parties and never participated in drinking, even though the legal age at the time was only eighteen. Christine was moving right along toward her goal, and nothing was going to stop her.

A Fateful Meeting

But this all changed in March 1968. Christine would walk at seven in the morning like clockwork. Always alone and always taking the same path, ending up at a local drugstore. Before visiting the store, though, she would meet with a group outside the local hospital for a smoke break. Niels Bjorn Jorgensen, a middle-aged medical resident, spotted Christine during one of these breaks.

Fresh from California, Niels was cocky, outspoken, and a bit peculiar. He didn't fit in with his peers. He was often an outcast for his odd behavior, such as carrying photographs of the slain Maori tribe whose massacre he claimed he had witnessed firsthand. This was one of many lies he told. Niels was the opposite of Christine. He never studied – furthermore, his roommate said he never had any mail or visitors. But the loaner, Niels, set his sights on Christine from their first meeting.

Christine felt uncomfortable around Niels despite his society-approved good looks and actively avoided him. This became harder as Niels became more and more obsessed. He followed her around campus, repeatedly asking her out – each time, she denied him. Around the time of the first rejection, Christine began receiving prank phone calls, in which she would answer and be met with silence on the other end. She also started seeing a man standing outside her dormitory window, forcing her to keep the shades closed nearly every hour of the day.

Niels could only withstand so many refusals from Christine. Before long, he became bitter and resentful, desiring to punish Christine for turning him down too many times. Soon, Christine's phone calls were no longer silent but filled with ominous messages. Then, she didn't just see a man – who she now knew was Niels – outside her window, but almost everywhere she went. By May 1968, Christine no longer thought Niels was harmless.

Her friend Linda noticed the change. She would always seem to be on edge and looking over her shoulder. Once Christine mentioned to Linda that she thought there might be more to Niels strangeness than just his social ineptitude. Still, she kept his stalking and harassment a secret from her friend. Thinking a transfer would solve her problem, she begged her mother in May

1968 to allow her to transfer to Vassar. Her mother resolutely refused.

At the end of a weekend visit, the last words Christine would say to her mother were "I hate you," several times.

A Horrific Campus Crime

Two days later, her mother changed her mind. Her parents decided they were going to surprise her at the end of the semester, in just a few weeks, with a huge party. Back on campus in Madison, Christine was livid. Riled up from the confrontation with her mother, when she saw campus police officers Tiny Frey and Roger Golemb, she decided to report Niels' abuse right then and there. If her mother wouldn't let her leave, at least she wouldn't have to suffer any longer.

However, the officers, namely Tiny Frey, didn't believe her. They told her to buy a whistle for her safety and never even filed a report on Christine's statement about the month and a half of stalking by the third-year medical resident. Christine was popular and pretty, and Tiny disregarded her confession on Monday, May 20, 1968, as the price she paid for her good looks.

Linda and Christine had plans to go to the Saturday swim meet, but at the last minute, Linda decided to travel home to Milwaukee for the weekend. Early Friday morning, she phoned Christine to let her know about the change of plans, but there was no answer. Linda glanced at the clock and realized her friend must have been out on her routine morning walk. Linda left a message and departed for her parent's house.

After a weekend of writing her term paper, Linda spent Sunday night readying herself for school in the morning. The next day, Monday, May 27, she was startled out of her last-minute preparations by a phone call at two-fifteen in the morning. Groggily, she picked up the receiver – surprised to hear a campus police officer on the other line. Officer Hendrickson introduced himself, then shocked her with news that would change her life forever.

He wanted to know the last time Linda had seen Christine and pressured her to tell him if Linda knew of anyone who had wanted to date Christine. Linda suspected that someone could have spiked Christine's drink, and she feared the worst, that perhaps her friend had been sexually assaulted. However, the morning news confirmed that the officer's call was regarding something much worse – Christine was dead.

The statement read: "A University of Wisconsin co-ed, Christine Rothschild, had been murdered."

On Sunday, May 26, a young boy was on an evening drive with his brother and parents on North Charter Street. As the car rolled through the city blocks, the boy called out from the back seat that he thought he had just seen someone lying in the bushes just outside Sterling Hall on campus. His parents continued on, figuring the boy's eyes betrayed him or that he had seen a mannequin as part of some bizarre college prank.

At seven-thirty in the evening, another student who lived in Sterling Hall, Phil Van Valkenberg, leaned over the railing to tap on his friend's window below him, coming face to face with the bloody and bruised body of a young woman.

Officer Golemb was first on the scene, followed quickly by his superiors and other campus detectives. They quickly assessed the body and collected as much evidence as they could. Almost immediately, Golemb recognized that the battered corpse was none other than Christine Rothschild, the young co-ed who reported a stalker to him and Officer Frey just six days earlier. However, their failure to previously file a report deterred them from coming forward to say anything about the girl's charge of harassment.

The medical examiner at St. Mary's hospital noted that her coat, dress, and boots were heavily coated in blood. Her jewelry remained, making robbery an unlikely motive. The coroner determined that a surgical scalpel had punctured Christine's chest and neck fourteen times. One of these stabs was a direct blow to her heart, killing her, after which the killer strangled her with a piece of fabric. After death, the killer had also taken the time to shove each of her gloves far down her throat, lodging them in her windpipe. In doing so, her jaw was broken, as were several of her ribs. Spinach in her stomach alluded to her death – around seven in the morning.

When Linda returned to campus, she and the other co-eds were on edge. Many of the girls who were not picked up by their parents were equipped with whistles and mace. Final exams were waived because students were terrified to leave their dorms.

Stained pants recovered from the crime scene had been sent to the FBI but returned no conclusive evidence. Christine's body was laid to rest on Wednesday, May 29, 1968. Her parents never got to share the good news of their approval of her transfer to

Vassar. The brutality and senselessness of her murder, which took place on the campus Christine had desperately begged to leave, tormented her parents for the rest of their lives. Her mother sank into a depression, turning Christine's bedroom into a shrine. They refused updates on her case and never discussed the crime with anyone.

A Decades-Long Hunt for a Killer

Detectives and police officers from multiple agencies conducted fifteen hundred interviews over the next two years – each one inconclusive. The police chief initially suspected that someone from the nearby hospital would have had to have seen or heard something at shift change the morning of the murder, but no one ever came forward.

Even though they continued investigating for a few years, some officers deemed the case cold within just a few weeks. Linda did come forward, but officers didn't pay her mention of Niels much mind. The following year, when she was a sophomore, Linda felt increasing pressure to make Niels' transgressions known. She sent a letter to campus police and called, but no one ever responded to her. Filled with embarrassment and shame for not doing more for her friend and having officers disregard her so flippantly, Linda vowed to expose Niels Jorgensen.

Linda graduated, got her master's, and eventually became a teacher. When she married her husband, she relocated to Texas. Each move and career change did not dissuade her from investigating Christine's case. She kept in touch with officers and former students and once even tracked down Niels himself. The floundering med student had been fired from his Madison residency on Monday, May 27, 1968, and had since moved to New York City.

Whether it was a coincidence, or Niels wanting to distance himself from the crime, may never be known. When Madison detectives flew to New York to interview Niels, they were met with deception and lies. While on route to the NYPD station to be interviewed, Niels claimed he felt very ill. As he had been so willingly and cooperative to come in in the first place, detectives turned around and dropped him back off at his apartment, telling him they would pick him up the next morning. The following day, Niels was gone.

He spent the rest of his days in California, living with his mother, who had long believed Niels had killed his brother in a diving incident around a decade earlier. He adamantly denied all charges of murder and told Linda that he never even knew of "that Rothschild girl."

Christine's murder has never formally been solved, and the University of Wisconsin-Madison and the surrounding area have largely forgotten. But the terrible memories live on in Linda's mind, and she has made it her lifelong mission to expose Christine's killer.

X

Adolph Coors III

KIDNAPPINGS FOR RANSOM STARTED TO increase during the 1960s. However, chillingly, most of them concerned the snatching of children. But that was not the case for the forty-five-year-old heir of the Coors brewing family. An unfortunate road closure provided just the opportunity one kidnapper and killer needed to strike a deadly blow.

The Heir

The Coors family was one of the most prolific brewing families in the United States. In the late 1800s, Adolph Coors was a German immigrant who had just landed in America. He moved to Colorado for the renowned fresh water, perfect for brewing beer. With time, the company grew, eventually being handed down to Adolph Coors II and finally Adolph Coors III. The third heir to the Coors company was the founder's grandson and, at forty-four years old, was also the CEO and chairman of the board.

He had attended the Phillips Exeter Academy in New Hampshire, one of the most prestigious boarding schools in the world. After which, he graduated from Cornell University, earning high honors.

After being schooled and trained for his inheritance, Adolph and his wife, Mary, settled down in Colorado with their four children, not far from the Coors headquarters. His brothers ran the operations alongside him, all living and working in Morrison, Colorado, in the 1960s. Adolph III was not the epitome of a high-powered businessman. He was a down-to-earth rancher at heart; he loved to hunt, fish, and raise cattle. His passion was the land; even though he loved his family's brewing company, he hoped to retire young and enjoy the ranch.

The Murder

Adolph was forty-five years old on February 9, 1960. He awoke as he always did, bright and early, working out before sitting down for coffee with his wife. Before heading to the brewery at seven fifty-five, he took care of his horses on the ranch. After a final goodbye to his family, he set off in his white-over-turquoise International Harvester Travelall.

Typically, he had a straightforward twelve mile journey to work, but the roads had been closed for construction. This meant Adolph had to take a rural, gravel road for four miles to Turkey Creek Canyon to take a state road back to the highway.

Sometime later that morning, the local milkman was going about his usual route. Like Adolph, he was detoured to Turkey Creek due to construction. However, when he arrived at the bridge bypass, his path was blocked by a car. He attempted to move the vehicle, which was still running, to continue on his way, but something caught his eye. Next to the abandoned vehicle was a large, bold, red-brown stain on the bridge's railing. Below the ominous spot lay a discarded hat on the riverbank. Inside the car, the police saw similar stains.

Fearing the worst, he immediately alerted the local authorities when he made it back to town. Anyone that lived in the Morrison or Golden, Colorado communities would be able to recognize the vehicle on the bridge – it was Adolph Coors' white-over-turquoise International Harvester Travelall.

Regardless of the reasons behind the stains and the abandoned vehicle, police knew instantly that they were dealing with a high-profile case. The brewing family was well-known and well-to-do, Adolph himself being heir to a fortune somewhere in the millions.

Upon hearing of their CEO and family members' disappearance, the Coors family sprang into action. Adolph's father went straight to the FBI director, James Edgar Hoover. He requested that he do everything in his power to find his son – without delay. Authorities contacted Adolph's wife and secretary – the former hadn't seen Adolph since he left for work, and the latter said that he never showed up.

The hat on the bank below the bridge was identified as belonging to Adolph, but other than the car, it was the only piece of evidence to be found. Police were baffled as to what had befallen the brewing company's heir. Until the ransom note came.

On the afternoon of February 9th, Mary received a typed letter. It told her that her husband had been kidnapped and demanded five hundred thousand dollars in tens and twenties in exchange for Adolph's return. The missive warned: "Call the police or FBI: he dies. Cooperate: he lives."

The kidnapper further instructed her to place an ad for a tractor in the Denver Times in order to communicate covertly. She did as she was told, aside from informing the FBI about her movements, but the ad went unanswered. The investigation's questioning of neighbors had revealed one other clue. An out-of-the-ordinary 1951 canary yellow Mercury had been seen in the area lately. The vehicle and its driver stood out in residents' minds, even leading one of them to memorize a portion of the license plate, "AT" and "62" – police now had a suspect to find.

Diligent searching through databases allowed authorities to trace the car to a Walter Osborne, who up until recently had been an employee of a nearby Denver paint company. When they ran the prints from Walter's identification, they found that more than his vehicle was cause for suspicion. Walter wasn't Walter at all – he was a convicted murderer and escaped felon named Joseph Corbett, Jr.

Killer Turned Kidnapper

Joseph Corbett Jr. was often cited by his peers, parents, and teachers as being shockingly intelligent. He had an above-average I.Q., though his social skills were somewhat lacking. Despite this, his upbringing was average, the son of a newspaper editor and a homemaker.

However, his social mannerisms became erratic as a teenager, and his parents worried. Joseph would spiral further with the death of his mother, who suffered a freak fall from a balcony. After this devastation, Joseph left home, disappearing for months until he murdered a hitchhiker in cold blood in California. He was sentenced to life in prison for shooting the unassuming man in the head.

But Corbett had other plans. In 1955, he escaped from a minimum-security cell in Chino after serving only five years. Walter Osborne, a Denver resident and paint factory employee, was embedded into the community within a year.

When police showed up at his apartment a few weeks after the kidnapping, Walter was gone, having told his landlady he was heading to Boulder, Colorado, to finish his studies. It would soon be discovered that he had gone much farther than Boulder. Around the same time, authorities in Atlantic City, New Jersey, were called to a dump for a suspicious fire. There, they found a smoldering burnt-out car, specifically, a 1951 canary yellow Mercury whose plates matched those belonging to Walter Osborne also known as Joseph Corbett.

On March 30th, Joseph Corbett became a household name when he was placed on the FBI's most-wanted list. His picture appeared in newspapers, magazines, and posters worldwide.

Even though police now believed they had their man, hope was fading every day, which brought no response to Mary's ad and no further letters from the kidnappers. It would be extinguished entirely on September 11, 1960.

That evening, a pizza truck driver headed out to a dump situated at the Rocky Mountain foothills just southwest of Denver. He had intended to do a bit of shooting for target practice, but he was stopped in his tracks before he could even withdraw his firearm. On the edge of the trash pile lay a pair of pants, finely made. Inside, the waistband read: "Expressly for Mr. A. Coors, III." In the pocket was an extravagant pen knife with engraving glinting on the side – "A.C. III." The truck driver alerted authorities at once.

Police poured into the dump, and it didn't take them long to find human remains. Some five hundred yards away were bones, including a skull, and dental records confirmed they belonged to the brewing company heir, Adolph Coors III.

Bone fragments gave clues to his cause of death; he had been shot from behind at close range twice.

Police went from Colorado to Toronto and California to Vancouver, trying to catch up with Corbett. On October 29th, a man matching Corbett's description was reported in British Columbia and said to be driving a fire-engine red Pontiac car. The unmistakably flashy vehicle was followed to an apartment complex. When police knocked on Corbett's door, guns drawn, he swung it open to reveal himself, hands raised, palms facing outward, calmly saying, "I'm your man."

No one had witnessed the killing firsthand, but police had plenty to go on.

They had receipts of a typewriter purchased by Corbett, whose typeface matched that of the ransom note. There were witness statements from Corbett's former coworkers who alleged that he would often say he was "planning something big."

He wasn't lying. Corbett had been studying Adolph's movements for weeks, all from the front seat of his yellow Mercury. Corbett seized the opportunity after construction had closed the road, forcing the wealthy heir onto a rough and largely deserted gravel side road. The morning of the murder, he backed his yellow vehicle partway into some brush just before the Turkey Creek bridge. A pistol sat in his coat pocket; beside him, on the passenger seat, there were leg irons and handcuffs. He would convince Adolph to come with him one way or another.

At first, he pretended to be broken down, knowing the kind Adolph would likely stop to help, which he did. Adolph left the door open and the engine running, thinking he would be right back after offering the stranded driver a ride or the promise of a phone call. However, that was not to be. When Adolph approached, Corbett withdrew his pistol.

A tall man of solid stature, Adolph reached for the gun, grabbing Corbett's hand. The two wrestled over the weapon briefly, falling onto the bridge's rails, at which point Adolph's cap fell to the creek below. Adolph, equally matched with Corbett, then decided to try and make a run for it. As he was running back toward his vehicle, Corbett fired two shots. Even though Adolph was dead, Corbett still sent the ransom letter, but in the end, he decided to run.

On March 29, 1961, Joseph Corbett was sentenced to life in prison – yet again. And, once more, his sentence was cut short. The model prisoner was paroled in 1980. Corbett moved back to Denver and led a solitary and quiet life. He cut off all ties with his few remaining family members, never married, and had no children. His neighbors never even got more than a grunt from him. Once, he told his story to a reporter, claiming he was innocent, and the FBI had set him up.

On August 24, 2009, he was found with a self-inflicted gunshot wound to the head. It seemed, for years, he had been living in a prison of his own creation.

XI

Robinson Family (Good Hart Murders)

ALL FAMILIES HAVE SKELETONS IN THE CLOSET, but in this story that cliché term becomes terrifyingly literal. From the outside, the Robinson's seemed like your average upper middle-class family. Well-behaved children, a doting housewife, and a hardworking father. So, when terror struck their idyllic summer retreat, no one could have ever seen it coming. Except, perhaps, Mr. Robinson and his mysterious companion, Mr. Roeberts. This is the story of an ill-fated family and a vacation gone terribly wrong.

The Robinsons Relaxing Retreat

The lakeside community of Good Hart sits nearly at Michigan's northernmost point in the Lower Peninsula. Edged by the waters of Lake Michigan on one side and the Mackinac Bridge not even an hour north, it is an idyllic summer escape.

One family, the Robinsons, enjoyed the locale so much that they purchased a seasonal home in Good Hart. It was a simple cabin of logs and stone surrounded by tall pines. It was secluded from town, near the beach, not even visible from the main road. However, other cabins in the tiny resort area of Blisswood weren't far away. Neighbors knew the Robinsons as upstanding people, churchgoers who were pillars in their community.

Mr. Richard Robinson, who went by Dick, was a respectable businessman. He owned an upscale magazine named "*Impresario.*" Like his wife, he abstained from alcohol and never gambled. He supported local charities, like the opera, and was often seen dabbling with his watercolor paints in his free time. His wife, Shirley, was the most passionate homemaker, loyal to her husband and entirely devoted to her children – of which she had four, Richie, Gary, Randall, and Susan. All four kids were polite, kindhearted, and well-mannered. Despite their well-to-do upbringing, they were never troublesome or prideful.

In the summer of 1968, forty-two-year-old Richard and forty-year-old Shirley were excited to spend uninterrupted time with their children. The oldest, nineteen-year-old Richie, had been away at college, attending Eastern Michigan University, while sixteen-year-old Gary, twelve-year-old Randall, and seven-year-old Susan were all still home. On June 16th, they arrived at their cabin in Good Hart, traveling from their home in Lathrup Village, just outside of Detroit.

Once there, they met with their caretaker, Chauncey Bliss, who looked after the cabins when they went away. Chauncey had built the Blisswood cabins in 1956, and agreed to stay on tending to them even after they were sold. Unfortunately, the Bliss family had recently suffered a loss. Chauncey's young son was killed in a motorcycle accident not long before the Robinsons arrived. Having known Chauncey for years, Richard Robinson stopped by his home on June 24th to pay his respects. He left twenty dollars for flowers and, while talking to Chauncey, informed him that their cabin would require upkeep in the near future.

Richard said that he and his family were leaving for a short trip on June 26th. They were going to look at property in Kentucky and Florida and expected to be gone at least a couple of weeks. After a few final condolences, Richard headed back to his cabin, where his family was enjoying their rustic retreat.

A Summer Slaying

Near the end of July, a few other cabin guests gathered for their annual bridge party. As they were all Blisswood residents, they had invited their nearby neighbor, Shirley Robinson. Still, a note on the Robinson cabin door informed everyone stopping by that they wouldn't be home until July 7th. As the ladies settled in, one of them remarked upon the bad and rotten smell that floated through the open windows. A light breeze soon filled the neighboring cottage with a foul odor. One woman noticed Chauncey Bliss passing by and reported the smell to him.

No one had seen the Robinsons for several weeks, and Chauncey recalled their inter-state travel plans. He suspected that an animal, like a raccoon, had gotten trapped and died in the cottage's crawl space. Since the building was unoccupied, no one noticed the smell until the creature's corpse began rotting.

Walking around the property, he confirmed that the smell was definitely coming from inside the cabin.

Chauncey withdrew his master key and prepared himself for the wall of terrible smell he was sure to be hit with when he opened the door. Only, there was no way he could have been prepared for what actually lay waiting for him.

As the sturdy door swung open, the bright afternoon sunbathed the room in light, illuminating the body of a woman lying on the floor. Her legs were exposed from the knees down while the rest of her was covered by a blanket. Chauncey could barely make out other forms in the hallway before the smell and the swarms of flies became too much. Choking down bile, he fled the Robinson cottage and immediately called the police.

Each of the Robinson family member was found scattered throughout the cabin, as were puddles of congealed body fluids and bloody footprints that had long ago dried. Shirley, the mother, was in the living room, and police suspected that the precise positioning of her body was on purpose, an attempt to make the scene look like a sexual assault. However, forensic evidence showed that she had not been assaulted or raped. Her death resulted from a gunshot to the head from a .25-caliber gun.

The killer's footprints led police to the corpses of her family.
Richard was found lying over the hot-air register in the hallway
with a matching bullet hole in his head. But he also had a .22-
caliber slug in his chest, believed to have been fired from a semi-
automatic, and skull fractures believed to be caused by blunt force
trauma. Young, seven-year-old Susan was just a feet away from her
father. A bullet had obliterated her face while skull fractures
radiated outward from her forehead. Police believed both her and
her father were beaten with a hammer recovered at the scene. The
family's three sons weren't far away.

College student Richie was half in the hallway, half in the
bedroom, his legs extending out into the hall. He had multiple
gunshot wounds to his head. Gary was discovered lying on his
back in the bedroom where his brother lay across the threshold.
He had been shot in the back by a .22-caliber but also in the head
twice with a .25. His younger brother, Randall, was draped across
his father in the hallway. A rug, in a lavender color, obscured his
body from his shoulders to his upper thighs. What appeared to be
a gunshot wound glistened in his skull, but no bullet was ever
recovered.

It was clear the family had been murdered in cold blood, but
how? A bullet hole was found in the rear window; it matched the

.22 caliber slugs found in the bodies of the family. Police surmised that the killer had first fired through the window at Richard. Next, he entered the cabin using an unlocked door, where he found the defenseless family waiting. The remaining five Robinsons were all fatally shot, while Richard and Susan were also bludgeoned with a hammer.

For nearly a month, their bodies had laid where they had fallen – found in a severe state of decomposition, smothered in flies. No one had suspected anything was amiss as the Robinsons were killed on June 25th, one day before they were supposed to leave on their trip. Despite the fact that they were allegedly traveling, only one suitcase was partially packed. Plus, there was lots of food in the home. Playing cards were left on the table, the game rudely interrupted by murder.

The Investigation

Because Richard was the first to be killed through the rear window, it was believed that he was the primary target. Neighbors and even Chauncey were baffled as to why anyone would want to murder the Robinsons, but back home, people had a few ideas.

Police interviewed Richard's employees and uncovered some disturbing evidence. The company was in treacherous waters, even though he presented himself as a well-off businessman. Additionally, his books didn't quite add up. Family members and friends told police that Richard was always going on about some scheme and "deals in the works" that would make him fabulously wealthy. Those who worked with him said he was a tyrant, constantly "paranoid and secretive."

Even the Lutheran minister at the church they attended told authorities that Richard seemed to possess a split personality, the generous and kind father versus the neurotic dictator.

Before long, investigators understood why the numbers for "*Impresario*" weren't adding up. Joseph Scolaro III was Richard's right-hand man, and he left him in charge of the business when the family vacationed in Good Hart. Unfortunately, Richard's trust was misplaced in Joseph, as over the past few months, he had embezzled upwards of sixty thousand dollars.

On the morning of the murders, seventeen phone calls were placed between the two men. Joseph claimed that after their casual and cheerful conversations, he spent the day at a plumbing convention. However, when authorities interviewed witnesses, they found that it had rained all day at the convention, and very few attendees actually showed up. These witnesses couldn't recall seeing Joseph there. The one who said they had indeed chatted with him at the convention recalled the weather as being sunny. Joseph's then ex-wife informed authorities that they were married at the time of the murder. She remembers him leaving for work and not returning until around eleven that night, an odd occurrence for her husband.

Joseph was brought in for a nearly twelve-hour interrogation session, over the course of which he failed two polygraph tests. Authorities also found that Joseph was the owner of two semi-automatic .25 caliber Berettas, though he claimed he had given one to Richard. The remaining gun in Joseph's possession did not match the slugs recovered from the scene.

Confounded, police dug deeper. A pair of Joseph's shoes matched the bloody footprints at the scene, yet they couldn't definitively determine if they were indeed a match.

Investigators were sure that the phone calls on the day of the killing were regarding Richard finding out about the embezzlement. After which, Joseph left Detroit, drove up to Good Hart, and killed the Robinsons before anyone else could find out about his schemes. Joseph did have a period of twelve hours of unaccounted time that day, and along with the shoes and the gun, he was the prime suspect. However, his fingerprints were never recovered from the scene, and there were no eyewitnesses to the crime. In the end, the state prosecutor decided not to press charges on the grounds of insufficient evidence.

In 1973, Joseph Scolaro was found dead from a self-inflicted gunshot wound. A note beside him read: "I am a liar, a cheat, a phony, but I am not a killer. I am scared and sick."

Joseph's death effectively removed him from ever being charged, though he was the prime suspect. However, other leads were followed too.

Chauncey Bliss found himself under suspicion when police surmised that he felt slighted by Richard in the weeks after his son's motorcycle accident and took his revenge via murder. However, Richard expressed his condolences, and people remarked that the men were amicable. Chauncey himself seemed very shaken up after stumbling upon the bodies.

Another person of interest was "Mr. Roeberts," a friend of Richard's first introduced into the case when police uncovered a letter between the two men that was perplexing and odd. In the letter, Richard called Mr. Roeberts "my father" and signed off, "I'm looking forward with great anticipation and love to the day when we finally meet—soon, I hope. Always—your son Richard." The letter further detailed bizarre plans, including a man referred to as "Steamboat Joe," whom Richard met "at the place we decided." Police suspected that Mr. Roeberts had something to do with the grand plans Richard was always talking about, and maybe Steamboat Joe was Joseph Scolaro, but they could never identify "Mr. Roeberts."

On June 6th, Richard brought "Mr. Roeberts" to the New Hudson Regional Airport in Oakland County, claiming he was a wealthy financier who wished to strike a deal with them. Later, an elderly man with a monotone, robotic voice called, claiming to be Mr. Roeberts, followed by an excited Richard who wanted to know how the call went. He told the airport managers that he was heading to Good Hart on vacation, but the managers could contact Joseph Scolaro if they wanted to discuss the business transaction further. Detectives asked Joseph, "Who is Mr. Roeberts?"

To which he replied, "Beats the hell out of me." Similarly, Shirley told friends that "a man" would be coming up to stay with them in Good Hart before heading out with the family to check out some property down south. Could Richard have been waiting for Mr. Roeberts on the night of the murder?

The mind-boggling coincidences and connections didn't stop there. Investigators found that Richard had once been treated in Oakwood Hospital in Dearborn for suspected schizophrenia. Former secretaries came forward and claimed he had sexually assaulted them.

A Leavenworth prisoner wrote a letter to Michigan state police saying that he knew the killer of the Robinson family – himself and another convict who had been hired by none other than Joseph Scolaro to off the family for a handsome sum.

Curiously enough, six years after the murders in 1974, a car was found on a roadside in southern Michigan, abandoned. State police searched the vehicle, shocked to find a luggage tag in the glove compartment. The owner's name was inscribed on the back – it was Shirley Robinson. The car was traced to a Toledo dealership, where it had last been sold in 1966. But by this time, all leads went back to a dead end, literally – the deceased Joseph Scolaro.

One final theory is that it could have been the work of a known serial killer, John Norman Collins. The co-ed killer from

Eastern Michigan University attended at the same time as Richard Robinson's oldest son, Richie. The family was slain in the middle of a period when Norman was killing unsuspecting college coeds. But the killing of a family way up north didn't fit Norman's MO.

For many, including investigators who worked on the crime at the time, the case is closed. However, because Joseph Scolaro killed himself before he could be tried, Michigan law defaulted the case to "inactive."

In the end, no one truly knows what happened on that beautiful June day in 1968 on the peaceful waters of Lake Michigan – where six lives were ruthlessly ended. Just as the family waited in vain to be found in their cottage, they will likely have to wait a while longer for justice to be brought.

XII

Irene Garza

IRENE WAS A BEAUTY QUEEN TURNED SECOND-grade schoolteacher. Though her devout Catholic upbringing encouraged her to give to the poor, her donation of her time and talents was telling of Irene's big heart and utter kindness. Which is why when she disappeared from midnight mass, her community was left reeling.

Sometime later when her watery grave was discovered, the public descended even further into grief and terror. Sadly, it would be decades before her family and her community had answers to their questions – and they were plentiful. Especially those concerning a rather suspicious clergyman and his odd behavior.

A Bright Future

Irene Garza was born to Nicolas and Josefina Garza in 1934. McAllen, Texas, the town where she grew up, was a small southern town, just steps from the Mexico border. Though her parents weren't wealthy, they worked tirelessly to grow their dry-cleaning business. Within a few years, the tiny storefront had become profitable enough to move the Garza family across town. Even though Irene was now a resident of the affluent "North Side" of town, she never forgot her South Side roots.

An incredibly brilliant and talented student, Irene shined brightly at her high school, McAllen High. She was an intelligent student and the first Latina to perform as a head drum majorette. Equally as striking was Irene's beauty. She was captivating, with her thin profile, dark hair, and glamourous looks. In 1958, she was crowned Miss All South Texas Sweetheart. Then, after graduating, she became her school's homecoming queen while attending Pan American College.

Through it all, Irene remained steadfast in who she was. Formally, she taught second grade at one of the local elementary schools; however, she devoted her time to teaching recently immigrated students English on the South Side of town. Her first paycheck was spent purchasing supplies for the less fortunate families that lived on the wrong side of the tracks. At the elementary school where she worked, Irene was the secretary of the parent-teacher association; with so many obligations, she had little time for dating.

Despite this, she once told a friend that she was seeing "this Angelo-boy," who may not have been terribly attractive but was fiercely religious. Something close to Irene's heart because, unlike many of her "free-love" peers, Irene was also a devout Catholic, taking communion every day and often attending midnight mass at Sacred Heart Church. As a member of the Legion of Mary, Irene took her faith incredibly seriously, much to the chagrin of her parents, whom she still lived with. Irene loved working with children and longed for a large family of her own one day.

Despite Irene's seemingly outgoing nature and unnaturally good looks, she described herself as shy and quiet. Irene was close with only a few friends, one of them being her best friend, Maria Alicia Sotelo.

A Chilling Confession

On Saturday, April 16, 1960, Irene called Maria and invited her to a movie. Irene had plans to attend Holy Saturday confession, which began around seven in the evening. Maria agreed, and Irene hung up, then lifted the receiver once more to place another call. She dialed the number for Sacred Heart Church and asked to speak with Father Richard Junius, the priest whom she preferred to hear her confession. She also needed to talk with him about the upcoming Easter egg hunt she was preparing for the local families. However, it wasn't Father Junius that answered but John Bernard Feit, a visiting priest who made rounds at three parishes, one of them being Sacred Heart. Feit explained that Father Junius was already hearing confessions, but Irene was more than welcome to meet with him.

Irene headed out from her home, nearly a dozen blocks from Sacred Heart, and arrived at the church just before seven. There, she was met by Feit on her way to the confessional line. Together, the pair headed off to the rectory, the small parish house where Father Junius and other clergymen resided next to the church.

A little after eight that night, Maria headed home from the theater alone; Irene had never shown up. Maria figured she became involved in something at her church, knowing that her faith always came first, and decided she would call her friend tomorrow. By midnight, Irene's parents were equally as worried but similarly guessed that Irene had stayed for midnight mass. When the former beauty queen turned schoolteacher still wasn't home at three the next morning, her parents called the police.

A missing person report was filed right away. The first order of business was retracing Irene's steps, a path that ended at the Sacred Heart Church.

Irene was noticed wherever she went. Those waiting in line for confession the night of her disappearance recalled a few key details. Father Feit's line was moving incredibly slow, hampered by the priest's odd habit of regularly leaving the confessional, only to return a few moments later. Except for once, he did not return. Witnesses saw him intercept Irene at the doors; from there, the pair headed across the lawn to the rectory.

Around eight in the evening, three priests returned from the rectory, one of them being Feit. Irene was not with them. A fellow father said that over coffee after midnight mass, Feit remarked on Irene's appearance, saying that there was a young woman who had desired to have her confession heard in the rectory. Feit said he told her to go into the church and wait in line like the other members.

The same priests to whom Feit had explained the odd occurrence informed authorities that Feit had noticeable scratches on his hand that morning. One priest, in particular, Reverend Joseph O'Brien, was suspicious of Feit. Especially the fact that he made numerous trips that evening and night using the parish car, a vehicle that was typically reserved for visiting church members.

Meanwhile, police were searching the area surrounding the house and the church. Two blocks from Sacred Heart, Irene's car was located. On April 18th, a most terrifying trail was uncovered that continued for several hundred yards down McAllen Road. First, a passerby found Irene's purse, followed by her shoe a few yards away. Next came Irene's lace Mass veil, lying discarded on the grass. It was the first physical evidence discovered in connection with missing Irene Garza. Police escalated the case, resulting in the most extensive search the Rio Grande Valley had ever seen.

Facing his Fate

On Thursday, April 21, 1960, four days later, Irene's body was found. Miles from the stretch of road where her belongings were uncovered, Irene was discovered floating in a canal. Most evidence had been washed away, but her body still held secrets.

The coroner determined her time of death to be around seven thirty in the evening on Saturday, April 16th, the night of her disappearance. She had been beaten, raped, and finally suffocated to death before being dumped in the canal. Strangulation did not seem to cause her suffocation; instead, the coroner believed a cloth was placed over her nose and mouth.

Two priests from Sacred Heart identified the body in place of her devastated parents. The Garza family gathered together at Nicolas and Josefina's house; when police told the couple of their daughter's discovery, Josefina let out a "long awful moan from deep inside her body – almost like the howl of a wolf," said to be "like nothing they had ever heard or ever heard again."

In time, over five hundred individuals would be interviewed, and fifty polygraphs would be performed, but police suspicion never strayed far from John Feit. Any hair, fingerprints, or semen

belonging to her attacker had been washed away in the canal –
however, the murky pool did turn up one thing. When police
drained the canal, they found a photo slide viewer belonging to
Feit. They suspected that its cord had been tied around Irene's
body, used as a weight to try and hold it down. Near the viewer
were candlesticks emblazoned with the seal of Sacred Heart
Church. However, police never attempted to connect them to
Irene's bruising or injuries.

Evidence continued to stack up against Feit. One teenage
parish member told authorities that she had previously felt
uncomfortable around Feit. After her confession, he told her from
the secluded confines of the confessional, "I need to talk to you
after confession, so wait for me." She did not stay but returned
home immediately.

At another church, where Feit was in attendance, a girl
named Maria America Guerra was sexually assaulted while
kneeling at the communion rail. Feit was strongly suspected as the
attacker, but priests discouraged church members from spreading
gossip that a member of the cloth could commit such a crime. The
incident occurred three weeks before Irene's death.

When investigators questioned Feit, he denied having met with Irene. He explained away the scratches on his hand by saying that he was worked up from confession and had to drive around the parish car to cool down. However, he noticed how sweaty he was once driving and decided to change his clothes. Finding his building locked and himself without his key, he climbed up a tree into a second-story window and was scratched in the process. Later, he told police another story about breaking his glasses and having to scale the pastoral house, the bricks scratching him during his ascent.

U.S. Border Patrol Agent Harry Cecil interrogated Feit for twelve hours. The conversation ended with Feit stating, "You will never convict me of anything." When authorities turned up to examine the parish car, it had been thoroughly cleaned inside and out.

Investigators diligently worked to gather evidence against Feit, but he was soon transferred from Sacred Heart to Loyola University in Chicago, where he would study seminary.

Meanwhile, police were still working on both Irene's case and Maria's rape case. In 1962, the rape case was brought first, ending in a hung jury.

Feit didn't want to face a jury again, so he decided to plead no contest to a misdemeanor charge of aggravated assault – slapping him with a five hundred dollar fine but also his freedom.

After the case concluded, Feit bounced from position to position. He was once at Trappist monasteries at New Melleray Abbey, Dubuque, Iowa, and another Abbey in Missouri. At each, he was "counseled" for his previous missteps. At the Servants of the Paraclete in 1966, he was in charge of supervising other priests who had sexually assaulted church members, many of them children. He was in charge of determining when they could be released back into duty – a job he proved terrible at.

Feit left the priesthood in 1972, got married, and had three children. He became director of volunteers for the Society of Vincent de Paul in Phoenix, where he relentlessly advocated for the poor.

When Feit left the priesthood, those who once kept his secrets felt less inclined to do so. Reverend Joseph O'Brien, a father at Sacred Heart in 1960, told police and Irene Garza's cousin how Feit had once admitted to the murder – but at the time, various reasons kept him from reporting the confession to investigators.

Another man from the Abbey in Missouri, Dale Tacheny, recalled how Feit once told him he was "aroused by women with high heels who walked on hard floors, and that he had a sexual compulsion to attack women from behind, particularly when he knelt behind them in church."

To Tacheny, Feit detailed the events of that fateful night. After hearing Irene's confession, he "subdued her and took part of her clothes off from the waist on up and then fondled her breasts." After which he put her in the rectory basement. Feit finished hearing confessions, then moved Irene to his apartment. By then, it was early Easter Sunday morning. In his bathroom, he placed Irene in a bag; she protested, saying, "I can't breathe. I can't breathe." Feit left her there so that he could partake in Easter services; when he returned, she was dead.

Taking the parish car once more, Feit moved Irene's body to the trunk, patting her on the breast while remarking, "Everything will be OK."

Feit never told Tacheny the name of his victim, though Tacheny surmised due to the date of Feit's arrival at the Abbey. When Tacheny asked Feit why he wasn't in jail, he simply stated, "The church is behind me."

In April 2002, Tacheny told his story to the police. Irene's case, which had sat cold for over four decades, was reopened. By that time, however, police were reluctant to bring the case before a grand jury. They claimed early police work on the case was poor, there was no physical evidence, and O'Brien, a star witness, was suffering from dementia.

Feit, for his part, glumly said, "That man doesn't exist anymore."

It would be another decade before interest rose once again. With a campaign by District court judge Ricardo Rodriguez to unseat the district attorney who chose not to try Feit, justice for the Garza family took center stage. Rodriguez won, and Feit was arrested in February 2016.

The eighty-three-year-old was extradited from his home in Scottsdale, Arizona, and pleaded not guilty in Texas. Tacheny testified in a closed deposition. On December 7th, Feit was convicted of Irene Garza's murder. The next day, he was sentenced to life in prison.

Feit served three years after living as a free man for fifty-seven years. On February 12, 2020, he died in the W.J. Estelle Unit, just outside Huntsville, Texas.

The Garzas finally had justice, but the world would remain just a little darker, forever missing the young, intelligent, beautiful, and kind Irene who had shined so brightly.

Conclusion

OUR DEPLORABLE DETAILING'S OF CRIME FOR the 1960s have come to an end. Many of these chilling cases have since gone cold, leaving families without justice and killers without consequences. A handful of these murders have long been forgotten, only brought into the light when a modern crime possesses eerie similarities. Though for witnesses, victims' families, and the investigators who hunted the killers – the cases never die.

Anyone among us could be capable of kidnapping, killing, or any of these diabolical acts. You never know what skeletons a person keeps in their closet.

We hope you enjoyed reading these gruesome tales of death and getting to know a handful of murderers who defied the odds by living in plain sight, at least for a time.

We look forward to providing you with more accounts of each decade's most diabolical in future volumes.

References

"7. The Co-Ed Murders: Ann Arbor District Library." *7. The Co-Ed Murders | Ann Arbor District Library*, Ann Arbor District Library, n.d., https://aadl.org/aapd/truecrimes/7.

Anglis, Jaclyn. "He Slaughtered Eight Nurses in One Night: The Rampage of Richard Speck." *All That's Interesting*, All That's Interesting, 17 Jan. 2022, https://allthatsinteresting.com/richard-speck.

Bovsun, Mara. "The Case of Adolph Coors." *New York Daily News*, 9 Apr. 2018, https://www.nydailynews.com/news/crime/case-adolph-coors-article-1.384641.

Campion, Patrick. "Hidden in Plain Sight: Terror in Ypsilanti." *WEMU*, WEMU, 30 Oct. 2017, https://www.wemu.org/wemu-news/2017-10-30/hidden-in-plain-sight-terror-in-ypsilanti.

Colleen. "Misconduct. A True Crime Podcast: Larry Peyton and Beverly Allan on Apple Podcasts." *Apple Podcasts*, Apple , 1 Dec. 2019, https://podcasts.apple.com/in/podcast/larry-peyton-and-beverly-allan/id1191380648?i=1000458388997.

Deklein, Dirk. "The Kidnapping and Murder of Adolph Coors III." *History of Sorts*, 9 Feb. 2018, https://dirkdeklein.net/2018/02/09/the-kidnapping-and-murder-of-adolph-coors-iii/.

East, Michael. "Unsolved Mysteries: Murder in the Library-the Killing of Betsy Aardsma." *Medium*, The Mystery Box, 2 Feb. 2022, https://medium.com/the-mystery-box/unsolved-mysteries-murder-in-the-library-the-killing-of-betsy-aardsma-c916f7634785.

"Graeme Thorne Kidnapping." *Lottery Critic*, 20 June 2019, https://www.lotterycritic.com/lottery-winners/graeme-thorne-kidnapping/.

Ignacio Blanco, Juan. "John Norman Collins: Murderpedia, the Encyclopedia of Murderers." *John Norman Collins | Murderpedia, the Encyclopedia of Murderers*, CrimeLibrary, n.d., https://murderpedia.org/male.C/c/collins-john-norman.htm.

Kuklovskaia Elizaveta. "DP." *Amazon*, "Books by Mail" Pub. Co., https://www.amazon.com/dp/B01M6D8URV/ref=dp-kindle-redirect?_encoding=UTF8&btkr=1.

Leandro, Marcelo. "1960 Murders at Forest Park." *ZODIAC CIPHERS*, N/A, 20 Apr. 2013, https://www.zodiacciphers.com/zodiac-news/the-murders-at-forest-park.

Media, Evil Mob. "Evil Transgression on Apple Podcasts." *Apple Podcasts*, 1 June 2022, https://podcasts.apple.com/us/podcast/evil-transgression/id1497823718.

Mike. "EP74 – Richard Speck." *True Crime All The Time*, PodcastPro, 26 May 2018, https://www.truecrimeallthetime.com/index.php/2018/05/26/ep74-richard-speck/.

Montaldo, Charles. "Her Method of Murder Was Poison and No Child Was Safe, Janie Lou Gibbs." *ThoughtCo*, ThoughtCo, 30 May 2019, https://www.thoughtco.com/janie-lou-gibbs-972718.

N/A. "Crimelines True Crime – Betsy Aardsma – 49:05." *RadioPublic*, Basement Fort Productions, LLC, 9 June 2019, https://radiopublic.com/crimelines-true-crime-6rMDNW/s1!9e749.

N/A. "Going West." *Going West*, 2019, http://www.goingwestpod.com/.

Podles, Leon J. "Irene Garza." *Author Leon J. Podles : The Murder of Irene Garza Case Study*, Crossland Foundation, 19 Feb. 2008, https://podles.org/case-studies/Irene-Garza-Case-Study-page1.htm.

Priestland, Anna. "Case 75: Graeme Thorne - Casefile: True Crime Podcast." *Casefile*, Casefile True Crime Podcast, 7 Feb. 2021, https://casefilepodcast.com/case-75-graeme-thorne/.

Redden, Jim. "After 50 Years, Murders Still a Mystery." *Https://Joomlakave.com*, Pamplin Media Group, 27 Oct. 2010, https://pamplinmedia.com/component/content/article?id=38808.

Splash and Shama. "The Tea True Crime." *Audible.com*, Audible, 2 Jan. 2022, https://www.audible.com/pd/The-Tea-True-Crime-Podcast/B09PJZDPZS?ref=a_pd_Janie-_c1_podcast-show-details&pf_rd_p=df6bf89c-ab0c-4323-993a-2a046c7399f9&pf_rd_r=DX1WFTJMEC6DREM1YZQ2.

Wolchek, Rob. "Michigan Murders: 50 Years Ago, Terror in Ypsilanti Ends." *FOX 2 Detroit*, FOX 2 Detroit, 17 Sept. 2019, https://www.fox2detroit.com/news/michigan-murders-50-years-ago-terror-in-ypsilanti-ends.

Acknowledgements

This is a special thanks to the following readers who have taken time out of their busy schedule to be part of True Crime Seven Team. Thank you all so much for all the feedbacks and support!

Robert Upton, Angie Grafton, Alicia Gir, Anna Rohrbach, Ashlynn Stinson, Angela Brockman, Bambi Dawn Goggio, Casey Renee Bates, Kurt Brown, Barbara English, Kris Bowers, Cara Butcher, Joyce Carroll, Cory Lindsey, Deirdre Green, Clara Cortex, Nancy Harrison, Dannnii Desjarlais, David Edmonds, Debbie Hill, Debbie Gabriel, Diane, Larry J. Field, Linda J Evans, Huw, Jennifer Lloyd, Jennie, Jon Wiederhorn, Judy Stephens, Fran Joyner, Kay, Jennifer Jones, Laura Rouston, Jason, Michele Gosselin, Mark Sawyer, Monica Yokel, Marcia Heacock, Muhammad Nizam Bin Mohtar, Bonnie Kernene, Nicky McLean, Ole Pedersen, Kathy Morgan, Patricia Oliver, Rebecca Ednie, Robert Fritsch, Christy Riemenschneider, Shane Neely, Don Price, Tammy Sittlinger, Tina Bullard Tina Shattuck, Tina Rattray-Green, Tamela L. Matuska, Marcie Walters, Wendy Lippard

Continue Your Exploration Into

The Murderous Minds

Excerpt From List of Twelve Volume 1

I

Marjorie Orbin

"What this seems to be is a revelation of your very darkest side, ma'am," said Judge Arthur Anderson, as he stared at Marjorie Orbin during her sentencing hearing. "When that dark side is unleashed, it's about as dark as it gets," he continued.

The judge spoke these words from his bench on September 8th, 2004, in a courtroom in Phoenix, Arizona. It was the start of fall in Arizona, a welcome reprieve from the blistering heat of the summer. It was not only the torrid heat that ended however, but a dark chapter of this desert community's crime annals.

A Grisly Find

The residents of Phoenix enjoy a patchwork of preserved desert areas throughout the city. However, on October 23rd, 2004, the rugged beauty of the area was eclipsed by a morbid find at the corner of Tatum and Dynamite Road, in North Phoenix. The Phoenix Police Department's 911 call center received a panicked call from an individual who was hiking in the area.

Police quickly arrived at the desert location, and the hiker led them to a spot that was not far off from the residential streets that surrounded the reservation. When the officers reached the site, they instantly knew that this was not a routine call. Detective Dave Barnes, of the Missing Persons Unit, arrived on the scene minutes later. A putrid smell filled the air as Barnes walked toward a 50-gallon Rubbermaid bin. "As we walked up you could smell the death in the air. Once you smell it, you know what it is for the rest of your life...it's the first time I had ever seen anything like that, where it's – just a piece of body," he would later say.

Barnes removed the lid and carefully opened the black trash bag contained within. Inside the trash bag was the bloody, dismembered torso of an adult male. Barnes would later tell a reporter, "All of the insides, all of the internal organs, intestines were missing...I thought, 'Who could do this to a human being? Cut off his arms, his legs, his head?'"

The grisly find was located less than two miles from the home of Marjorie Orbin, who lived in the 17000 Block of North 55th Street. Butcher had a strong suspicion that he had just found the torso of her missing husband; Marjorie had filed a missing person's report on September 22nd, 2004.

Jay Orbin was the successful owner of Jayhawk International, a dealership that specialized in Native American Art. He frequently traveled for business purposes, and it was not unusual for him to be gone three weeks out of the month. It was through his business travels that Jay met Marjorie.

The Stripper and the Salesman

Marjorie had been married seven times before meeting Jay at the age of 35. Marjorie was unable to conceive children and had lived a life with herself as the central focus. She entered each relationship looking for her Prince Charming, but it never happened.

Michael J. Peter was a very successful businessman who had made millions creating upscale strip clubs around the world. Marjorie left Peter because she believed he was cheating on her.

She moved to Las Vegas, where she danced at a strip club. It was at this strip club in 1993 that she met Jay, who was traveling through Las Vegas. They had been dating for a while when Jay proposed to Marjorie, offering to pay for fertility treatments if she married him. Marjorie accepted Jay's proposal, and they got married at the Little White Wedding Chapel in Las Vegas.

Soon afterward, they moved to Phoenix, where Jay lived. Marjorie was able to conceive and gave birth to their son, Noah. The couple divorced in 1997 but continued to live together. Marjorie had problems with the IRS and did not want Jay's assets to be vulnerable.

Jay's Disappearance

September 8th, 2004, Jay was driving back to Phoenix from a business meeting when he got a call from his mother, wishing him a happy birthday. That call was the last time anyone spoke to Jay.

When Jay's parents, brothers, and friends called his home, Marjorie told them that he had gone on a business trip and would not be returning until September 20th. During that time, those who cared about Jay could not reach him on his cell phone. His parents and friends expressed their concern to Marjorie; however, she said she did not know what was going on with him.

People who spoke to Marjorie about Jay stated that she expressed little concern for his welfare. Jay's intended return date passed, and still, nobody could reach him. When they inquired with Marjorie, she continued to remain aloof to their concerns. After continued pressure from friends and family, a missing person's report was filed on September 22nd.

Suspicion is Raised

The Police Department assigned Detective Jan Butcher to the case. She interviewed Marjorie, who indicated that the last time she'd seen Jay was on August 28th, when he had attended his son's birthday. Butcher became suspicious of Marjorie on September 28th, after leaving voicemail messages for her before she called back. "I asked her to provide me the license plate of the vehicle Jay was driving. She said she would call me back. She never did. So, that was a little bit odd," she later told a reporter.

From that point on, Butcher's suspicions only continued to grow. Credit card and phone tower records indicated that Jay had arrived at his home in Phoenix on September 28th, which didn't match Marjorie's claim that she had last seen him on August 28th.

When detectives checked Jay's credit card records, they found that Marjorie was spending thousands of dollars, including purchasing a $12,000 baby grand piano, while the business account had a withdrawal of $45,000. Within one day of reporting Jay missing, she had liquidated a total of $100,000 from Jay's personal and business accounts.

A final cause for suspicion arose during a call that Detective Butcher made to Marjorie requesting that she take a polygraph test. Butcher heard Marjorie remark to someone in the background, "You know what? She wants me to take a polygraph tomorrow." A male voice replied, "You tell her to go f--- herself."

Butcher obtained a search warrant and went to Marjorie's home, accompanied by a SWAT team. The SWAT team forced their way in and encountered an adult male, Larry Weisberg. Larry was Marjorie's new boyfriend and the voice that had been heard in the background of the phone call. Weisberg was combative, resulting in police tasing him.

Police searched the premises and found a large number of credit cards belonging to Jay, plus his business checkbook, items that he always kept with him when traveling. Though police did not make any arrests, their surveillance of Marjorie deepened. It was shortly after Marjorie's home was searched that police found Jay's torso in the Rubbermaid bin in the desert.

DNA evidence confirmed the torso belonged to Jay Orbin. The Maricopa County Medical Examiner's Office inspected the torso and concluded Jay had been shot and his body frozen. At some point, the body had been defrosted, and a jigsaw was used to dismember and decapitate it.

When searching Jay's business, police found a packet of jigsaw blades, with some of the blades missing. The Medical Examiner's Office determined the blades from the business matched the cut marks on the torso, where the limbs and vertebrae were severed.

Detectives traced the UPC code on the Rubbermaid bin back to a Lowes Home Improvement store in Scottsdale. The detectives scored big when they viewed video from the store's surveillance cameras and saw Marjorie purchasing the Rubbermaid bin, trash bags, and black tape. Police detained Marjorie when they caught her forging Jay's signature while making a purchase at a Circuit City store.

Jay's remaining body parts were never found, nor the gun that was used to shoot Jay.

Marjorie and her boyfriend, Larry Weisberg, were arrested on December 6, 2004. Weisberg was offered immunity if he agreed to testify against Marjorie, who was sentenced to life in prison on October 1st, 2009.

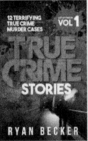

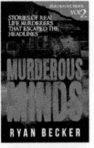

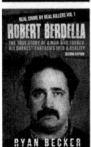
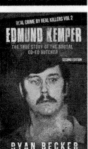

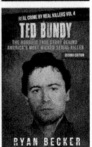

About True Crime Seven

True Crime Seven is about exploring the stories of the sinful minds in this world. From unknown murderers to well-known serial killers.

Our writers come from all walks of life but with one thing in common and that is they are all true crime enthusiasts. You can learn more about them below:

Ryan Becker is a True Crime author who started his writing journey in late 2016. Like most of you, he loves to explore the process of how individuals turn their darkest fantasies into a reality. Ryan has always had a passion for storytelling. So, writing is the best output for him to combine his fascination with psychology and true crime. It is Ryan's goal for his readers to experience the full immersion with the dark reality of the world just like how he used to do it in his younger days.

Nancy Alyssa Veysey is a writer and author of true crime books, including the bestselling, Mary Flora Bell: The Horrific True Story Behind an Innocent Girl Serial Killer. Her medical degree and work in the field of forensic psychology, along with postgraduate studies in criminal justice, criminology and pre-law, allow her to bring a unique perspective to her writing.

Kurtis-Giles Veysey is a young writer who began his writing career in the fantasy genre. In late 2018, he has parlayed his love and knowledge of history into writing nonfiction accounts of true crime stories which occurred in centuries past. Told from a historical perspective, Kurtis-Giles brings these victims and their killers back to life with vivid descriptions of these heinous crimes.

Kelly Gaines is a writer from Philadelphia. Her passion for storytelling began in childhood and carried into her college career. She received a B.A. in English from Saint Joseph's University in 2016 with a concentration in Writing Studies. Now part of the real world, Kelly enjoys comic books, history documentaries, and a good scary story. In her true crime work, Kelly focuses on the motivations of the killers and backgrounds of the victims to draw a more complete picture of each individual. She deeply enjoys writing for True Crime Seven and looks forward to bringing more spine-tingling tales to readers.

James Parker the pen-name of a young writer from New Jersey who started his writing journey with play-writing. He has always been fascinated with the psychology of murderers and how the media might play a role in their creation. James loves to constantly test out new styles and ideas in his writing so one day he can find something cool and unique to himself.

Brenda Brown is a writer and an illustrator-cartoonist. Her art can be found in books distributed both nationally and internationally. She has also written many books related to her graduate degree in psychology and her minor in history. Like many true crime enthusiasts, she loves exploring the minds of those who see the world as a playground for expressing the darker side of themselves—the side that people usually locked up and hid from scrutiny.

Genoveva Ortiz is a Los Angeles-based writer who began her career writing scary stories while still in college. After receiving a B.A. in English in 2018, she shifted her focus to nonfiction and the real-life horrors of crime and unsolved mysteries. Together with True Crime Seven, she is excited to further explore the world of true crime through a social justice perspective.

You can learn more about us and our writers at:

truecrimeseven.com/about

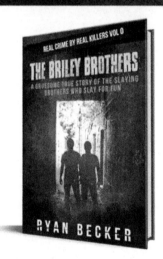

Dark Fantasies Turned Reality

Prepare yourself, we're not going to **hold back on details or cut out any of the gruesome truths...**